I Love Baja!

Pursuing The Dream Of Retiring And Living In Mexico

Written By

Mikel K Miller

Includes Appendices about Costs of Living,
Mexican Health Care, and Real Estate Risks

I Love Baja!

$14.95 US

Front cover photo: Pacific Ocean at Plaza del Mar, Km57,
Rosarito, Baja California, courtesy of Kirk and Bernice Hallam and
Gregg.

Photo credits: p. 14-Vickie Chantlos; p. 58-Ruben Mireles; p. 149,
155-Debbie Gobe; p. 225-Nadine Lockitch. All other photos by
the author, except for photos in the public domain.

ISBN: 144993224X
EAN-13: 9781449932244

To Lauren and Bill—the first to encourage me
to write about my Baja journey.

And for Debbie and Sandy–
good Baja neighbors and great friends.

Acknowledgments

Thanks to everyone who helped make this book a reality.

The name of the book comes from people telling me how they feel about the Baja peninsula in Mexico. On my trip to "the Baja" in January 2006, everybody I met said they loved the place and the people. When I told friends back in the USA about the trip, people who had visited Baja said they also loved it. Since then, hundreds more people have told me the same thing. I love it too.

Family and friends back in Maryland read the 2008 draft manuscript. A few other friends and writers in the USA read the draft 2009 manuscript. Hope and Adrienne, my "unofficial copy editors," suggested important improvements.

Several people who have firsthand knowledge about life in Baja also gave me valuable feedback. Almost all the Baja residents mentioned in the book vetted the anecdotes involving them. Debbie and Sandy—the "crazy women" in the prologue—reviewed some chapters as I wrote. Rosella and Rosemary, my trusted Mexican *amigas*, helped with phrases and words *en español*. Susan had some suggestions for the next-to-final draft manuscript, as did Graham.

Fellow members of the Baja Writers Workshop provided the most significant feedback during 2009 and 2010, discussing selected chapters at our weekly workshop meetings. Marsh and Lynnsie reviewed the final draft manuscript. More than eighty people from Baja and the USA saw parts of the manuscript in one stage or another.

Special thanks to Rafael for designing the cover and to Nathan for formatting the interior layout and pictures to send to the printer. Thanks also to Lauren, Brad, Vilma, and Nancy for reviewing the printer's proof copy.

Table of Contents

I Love Baja!

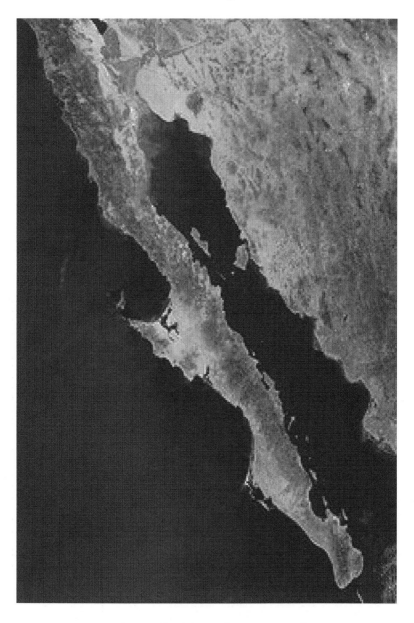

NASA Satellite Photo of Baja Peninsula
http://en.wikipedia.org/wiki/Baja_California_peninsula

Introduction

This book covers two life-changing events—retiring, and living in a foreign country. The overall theme is about adapting to life outside the USA, making new friends, and becoming part of the local culture.

Anecdotes from my observations and personal experiences in Baja fill the book. "Crazy Women and Stray Dogs" (the Prologue) provides a glimpse of expatriate life in Baja with friends and neighbors. "*Papá* Swims With the Whales" (Chapter 6) is about my taking three Mexican women and their young children on a three-day trip to see migrating whales.

I used to dream of living in a great year-round climate by the ocean and the mountains. I found that place in Baja. The Pacific Ocean, the mountains, the Sea of Cortez, and the rugged desert terrain sustain me. The people and the experiences we share enrich my life.

During Christmas 2007, my daughter-in-law Lauren suggested I write about some of the experiences. In May 2008, I told the story of *Papá* and the whales to my wife Nancy and family friends Bill and Sharon. Bill said I should write a book.

Spending much of my time in Baja after retiring, I rediscovered the joy of daily writing, which was my first profession as a journalist. Writing this book was like painting a picture of life in Baja using sentences and paragraphs as brush strokes. The paragraphs became anecdotes, stories, chapters, and then a book. All the anecdotes are from real events and use the real names of people involved—except for some who want their names withheld.

Sometime late in 2008, friends started introducing me to others as somebody who was writing a book about Baja. One stranger in Baja asked if I had read Jack Smith's book *"God and Mr. Gomez."* Another said I should read Graham Mackintosh's epic *"Into a Desert Place."* Still another suggested Marsh Cassady's book *"Baja y Yo."* However, I waited to read all of them until I finished my draft manuscript so other Baja books would not influence my writing.

I was relieved to see Smith's 1974 book is distinctly different from mine. For starters, a lot has changed in Baja since he published his book. Mackintosh's 1988 account of his 3,000-mile walk throughout Baja is incomparable. Cassady's 2008 book is more like mine—a collection of anecdotes, short stories, and feature articles. I joined his Baja Writers Workshop in 2009, and I continue to learn about writing from him and other workshop members.

Hopefully, you will enjoy reading about life in Baja as much as I enjoy Baja. And maybe you'll like *"I Love Baja!"* much as I like *"God and Mr. Gomez,"* or *"Into a Desert Place,"* or *"Baja y Yo."*

~ Mikel Miller, Baja California, Mexico, June 2011

Prologue:
Crazy Women and Stray Dogs

There is nothing like a good roadtrip to remind me how much I enjoy Baja. I've taken several of them on the Baja peninsula with many friends. I hope to take many more.

In early 2010, I began planning my annual whale-watching adventure in Baja. Right away my Baja neighbors Debbie and Sandy wanted to go too. Other friends and neighbors in the La Misión area started talking about going and it seemed we might have a convoy of two or three vehicles. A week before the trip the number of confirmations dwindled to six of us—just enough to fit comfortably in my Suburban with three rows of seats.

The first morning whale encounter at Scammon's Lagoon was great, with more whales than I saw during trips the previous two years. Mother whales and their calves swam alongside our 23-foot *panga* and dived under it. Dozens of others breached and flipped their tails within easy camera range. Our little boat was a mini international cruise ship with an Italian graduate student and her friend, plus a professor from Mexico City.

I Love Baja!

Afterward I was standing in the *Casa El Viejo Cactus* gift shop in Guerrero Negro, talking with Elena the manager about my forthcoming book. A stranger interrupted us and wanted to confirm who I was.

"Are you the guy writing that funny book about Baja?" she asked. A question such as that is sweet music to a writer's ears. I confirmed her notion. She introduced herself as somebody who lives in Punta Piedra near La Misión, and said some of her neighbors told her about my stories involving people in the area.

"Are you on one of your trips with those crazy women from Plaza del Mar?" she asked. She explained that she knew Debbie and Sandy, whom some people have dubbed Thelma and Louise. I surmised that she meant adventuresome, but I understood crazy too. I said yes.

Just then Debbie and Sandy showed up, followed closely by Annelise and Vickie. We invited her to join us for our usual wine and cheese at the end of a day on the road. However, she had to get back to her husband at a nearby motel and go to dinner.

We walked back to our rooms at the Malarrimo motel adjacent to the gift shop. A recent Midwestern retiree on the trip with us—let's call him "Frank"—was already a glass into a bottle of good Chilean Burgundy. The breezeway with the bougainvillea arch between our rooms made a good spot to pull up some chairs and a couple of tables. We spread out the cheese, crackers, apples, and plates. Frank gave us a lesson about the French origins of Burgundy wine from Chile, and we began chatting about our whale-watching trip that morning.

Debbie befriended a stray female dog she found hanging around the motel. She cuddled it to keep it warm in the late afternoon breeze. Sandy got a sweater from her room to keep it from shivering. We uncorked another bottle of Chilean wine. Everything was pretty mellow until Debbie said she wanted to take the dog back with us and find it a home in the USA.

I don't own dogs or cats, primarily because I don't want the responsibility. Frank apparently has the same philosophy. He was scowling and I could see he was giving me a look that said no-way-in-hell. I could also see the four women were enthusiastic about the idea of rescuing yet another stray, oohing and aahing over the dog. Debbie said she would have it checked out at a vet before we left, get it a flea bath, and get it vaccinated. I said okay.

"Great," she said. "I bought a carrying case while you were buying wine and cheese." Frank scowled even more.

They started choosing a name for the stray dog and Frank looked more dejected and pained. They teased him that they should call her "Frances" in his honor. It didn't win any points with him. They added a second name, calling her Frances-Ann. That didn't please him any better. He gave up and retreated to his room. We ran out of the good wine and had to break into our reserve for a $2 bottle of Merlot from Wal-Mart.

The conversation turned to sex, as it often does among expats who live alone. Vickie had chatted with a trio of male sightseers in the gift shop and asked them to join us. Too bad they didn't come by, she said. One had a camera strap around his neck with his camera lens dangling down, and she said it was "really big." All the women laughed.

The not-very-tall professor who was in our whale-watching *panga* did come by. After he left, everybody agreed he couldn't take his eyes off Sandy's ample bosom. She said he might be "a little short" for her and they laughed again. They love a good double-entendre, or a bad pun. After several more one-liners and more laughs, I joked that they were having "oral sex"—talking about it rather than doing it. All of us laughed at that.

A chilly 20-knot wind the next morning canceled our second whale-watching trip. Frank decided to catch a bus home because he didn't want to ride back with a stray dog. Besides, he said, Frances-Ann probably would puke and poop and piss all over everything.

I drove him to the bus station a few blocks away, where we learned the bus wouldn't let him off at La Misión. He chose the 11 o'clock bus for Ensenada and said he would call friends in La Misión to meet him. He didn't have enough pesos and the clerks didn't take US dollars. They just looked at him when he pulled out his Visa card. I gave him some pesos in exchange for some of his dollars and he had a ticket in his hand when I left. However, he didn't make the bus and showed up back at the motel about 11:30 a.m.

"They canceled it," he said in disbelief. The next one would leave at 2 p.m. and arrive in Ensenada at midnight.

He was determined to go his own way and declined to go with the rest of us on an afternoon trip to the town plaza in San Ignacio. After touring the impressive church, we enjoyed fresh bread made with local dates and found a little sidewalk cafe where we had ice cream and Mexican *café*. Debbie wondered how Frank was doing, riding ten hours on a Mexican bus with some passengers maybe holding dogs on their laps.

I laughed so much it hurt.

The next morning, without Frank to jerk around, they shortened the dog's name to Annie, as in Orphan Annie. She puked once while we were going through the winding curves in the mountains, but the bath towel in her carrying cage contained it. She never pooped or pissed, and seemed to get used to the motion after a stop at a military checkpoint. Overall, she was a good traveler and napped on the third row seat with Debbie, her paws up in the air sometimes.

We stopped for a late lunch in El Rosario at Mama Espinoza's, an iconic roadside cafe dating to 1934. The Internet has various ages for her, but the book "*Baja Legends*" says she was born October 16, 1910.[1] We didn't get to meet her and I had to settle for buying a copy of her autobiography and some T-shirts. We feasted on Margaritas

---

[1] Baja Legends; Niemann, Greg; Sunbelt Publications; San Diego, CA; 2002; p. 149

and lobster, had more "oral sex," and found a great little motel called the Baja Cactus to spend the night.

Before leaving El Rosario, Sandy wanted to go back to a community museum she and Debbie visited three years earlier. They found it on a trip by themselves while exploring dirt roads between Route 1 and the ocean. In fact, they took so many dirt roads they made it only as far as El Rosario on the six-day trip—just five hours from home. They were trying to find a petrified forest described in Debbie's tourbook, giving up after wading halfway across a river that kept getting deeper and deeper. Just another example of why some people refer to them as crazy women.

Sandy remembered the museum was down a dirt road. All the roads are dirt and she wasn't sure which one. We chose one that looked familiar to her and bumped along until we decided we were lost. I stopped and asked for help from a *señorita* walking on the roadside.

"Donde esta el museo?" I asked, stumbling over my *español* verbs and pronunciation. Vickie tried it too because she knows more *español* than I do. *La señorita* turned and pointed toward the river in the distance.

"It's over there," she said in good *inglés*. "This road is bad. Go back to the good road."

The good road soon turned into a rutted trail along the riverbank, with no museum in sight. We flagged down a small delivery truck bouncing toward us and tried our *español* again. The two guys seemed to understand what we asked, but just shook their heads. Maybe they had never been to the *museo*.

"Esta camino bueno?" Vickie asked, trying to learn if the road was good enough for us.

"Si," the driver replied. *"Esta bueno."* A little farther, the good road ended at the river. The only apparent option was to cross it.

"No way," said Annelise. A rusty little SUV with Mexican plates went past us, splashed through the water, and emerged on the other side. We made it too.

We found the little *museo* farther down the river, across the road from the ruins of an original mission dating to the 1700s. The display inside explained we were on *El Camino Real* - known as The King's Highway - built to link missions throughout the Californias. Graham Mackintosh walked the route in his classic book "*Journey With a Baja Burro.*"

Near Colonet, we decided to stop and take pictures at the four ocean lots Debbie, Sandy, and Bobbie bought on former *Ejido* land. They discovered the land while exploring those dirt roads. We found the correct dirt road this time and bumped along it for more than three miles heading toward the ocean.

Debbie (l), Sandy (r), and Author near Colonet – Photo by Vickie Chantlos

The late afternoon sun painted the landscape with soft colors, accenting the green fields full of yellow blossoms. Cattle and goats and horses roamed the wide open land; a couple of youths raced bareback on horses across one field. About a mile beyond the cluster of *Ejido* homes, the ocean was beautiful, waves lapping at the sandy shoreline of their lots. It was so peaceful. The three of us posed together for Vickie to take a picture capturing the moment, the sun on our left shoulders, the ocean behind us.

One of the funniest "oral sex" stories on the trip is the one Sandy and Debbie tell about needing to have a tire repaired and stopping at the little *llantera* in La Misión—the roadside tire shop that also offers to repair automatic transmissions. Sandy tells the story with gusto. Debbie interrupts to add details now and then.

The owner wasn't there. They spotted a *hombre* working amid some junked cars below the edge of the hill, and shouted down to him using combined *inglés* and *español* to ask about the shop owner. He pointed to the owner's *casa*. The owner showed up in a few minutes acting as if he didn't understand *inglés* very well either. He understood what was wrong with the tire, however, and began working on it. They watched him, standing just a few feet away.

They started talking about the guy down among the cars. Debbie says he was really good-looking, muscular, and wearing a sleeveless shirt. He was using a welding torch on something, and Sandy says he was hot in more ways than one. They took turns describing to each other what they would like to do with him, right there, right then. They were laughing and talking loudly and their fantasies became more and more vivid.

After the guy from the *llantera* repaired their tire, he walked over to the edge of the hill and hollered down to the *hombre*. Debbie says the guy walked up the embankment to join them. Turns out the tire shop owner understood *inglés* very well and he told the guy what they said about him.

Sandy says the hot *hombre* took off his sweaty shirt to reveal his pecs and abs. Debbie poses and postures, showing how he flexed his muscles for them. He spoke something *en español*, which the *llantera* owner translated for them.

"You ladies want to party?" he said the hombre wanted to know.

"No, no, no," they said, laughing with embarrassment. Then they retrieved their tire, jumped into their car, and sped off. They still laugh about it.

As I said in the beginning, a good roadtrip reminds me of how much I enjoy Baja. Especially if it includes whales, crazy women, and "oral sex."

Chapter 1:

The Journey Begins

A Chinese proverb says a journey of a thousand miles begins with a single step. In January 2006, I took my first serious step in looking for a vacation place during retirement.

It had to be on a coastline, because something about oceans makes me feel better—walking on a beach, listening to waves crashing on the shore, or just looking out to the horizon. Maybe I could find a place with a comfortable climate all year.

My wife Nancy and I had been to many coastline locations over the years from Maine to Louisiana, the Caribbean, San Diego to Seattle, and Hawaii. However, most had drawbacks—high costs of living and high population densities; too cool in winters, too hot in summers; heat, humidity, and hurricanes; mosquitoes and other insects.

She suggested I check out the San Diego area again, which I had liked immediately on my first visit in 1975. News stories on the Internet said the housing boom in the USA had spilled over into northern Baja. CBS aired a feature on "60 Minutes" about what was happening. It was becoming much like a new part of the San Diego suburbs south of the border, with the ocean and mountains and a similar climate, and a cost of living far less than the USA. Also, it's only an hour or so by car from medical centers and the San Diego airport.

I first visited Baja during Memorial Day weekend in 1980, enjoying lobster at Puerto Nuevo and staying in an oceanfront cottage in Ensenada with friends. The lifestyle and people were casual back then, and I was anxious to learn if Baja still had that good feeling. To find out, I scheduled an exploratory trip to the northern Baja coast.

The place I stayed was a tiny two-room rental cottage in the hills above the small village of La Misión, about forty miles south of the border. A winter rainstorm delayed my arrival, I lost my way after dark, and I had to find a roadside phone to call Lynn, the caretaker. She agreed to drive down from the hills to rescue me. I asked how I would recognize her.

"I drive a Jeep with Canadian tags, and I'm the only blue-eyed blonde in town," she said. Soon I spotted her muddy SUV.

In the daylight, I began noticing all the new construction along the Pacific Ocean. Construction crews were scraping shacks and old buildings off the coastline along Route 1. In their place, developers were building condos and houses, shopping centers and restaurants. Wal-Mart, Costco, McDonalds, Starbucks, Domino's, and Subway were already in northern Baja. Home Depot, another Wal-Mart, Applebee's, Burger King, and a second multiplex movie theater were in the works.

Retirees—maybe 20,000 already—were moving into the sixty-eight-mile stretch of coastline that realtors and developers dubbed the Baja Gold Coast. Retiring Baby Boomers might double or triple that number in just a few years as they began looking for less expensive places to retire. The U.S. State Department said about half of all USA retirees already living in foreign countries lived in Mexico.

Despite the boom, northern Baja had much of the same laid-back feel of my weekend a quarter century earlier.

Sure, the Puerto Nuevo lobster village had grown, and I couldn't find the same little *casita* overlooking the bay in Ensenada. But I found what I wanted.

The climate, the ocean, and the mountains rejuvenated me. The clean sixty-degree fresh air blowing right off the Pacific Ocean felt just right in the daytime sun. Millions of stars filled the nighttime skies over the ocean, constellations clearly visible without city lights to obscure them. I enjoyed some short sightseeing trips with Lynn and her mother, taking the back way over the beautiful hill country and visiting the bustling cruise ship waterfront in Ensenada.

After two weeks, my boss back in Maryland became anxious about deadlines and I had to cut my visit short. I spent most of the next eighteen months planning for retirement, visiting Baja as often as possible.

Nancy and I separated in the fall of 2007, a few months before co-workers threw a Mexican-theme retirement party for me with a sombrero, sunshades, and a *piñata*; a Mexico guidebook and *inglés-español* dictionary; and lots of laughing. I loaded everything into my car and headed for Baja before another East Coast winter.

In Baja, I settled into the oceanfront community of Plaza del Mar about thirty-four miles south of the U.S. border among expatriates from the USA, Canada, South America, and Europe.

My new life had begun.

I Love Baja!

Chapter 2:
El Baile de la Mordida

La policia stopped me three times in just six days after I moved to Baja. They seemed to target my 2006 Dodge Charger.

Once, they said I ran through a stop sign on Benito Juarez Boulevard, the main street through Rosarito. I didn't.

Another time, a cluster of *policia motocicleta* pounced on me just before the bridge leading to San Diego and two of them insisted that I was speeding down the long hill from *Playas de Tijuana* to the bridge. I wasn't.

A third time, they said I didn't signal a lane change going up the same hill. Probably I didn't.

Maybe it was because the USA license plate was like a blinking sign saying *TURISTA*. Maybe it was because Chargers were relatively rare in Baja in 2007. I think mostly it was because it was *un carro rojo*—not just any red car, but what Dodge calls Inferno Red. Whatever…they reacted to the car the same way a bull reacts to a fluttering red cape.

The first time *la policia* stopped me, on my exploratory trip in 2006, I was nervous and didn't know what to expect. Some of the things I had heard and read about Mexican justice ran through my mind—guilty until proven innocent, no lawyer, staying in jail until a judge's verdict, etc.

I Love Baja!

The policeman must have been right behind me when I made a U-turn at an intersection to pick up a carryout pizza at Domino's with my cousin Hope. The siren and lights started immediately. He spoke a little *inglés,* and said he would have to give me a ticket. He offered to let me pay him a $40 fine right there rather than making me go to the police station - *la comisaria* - to pay the fine.

"*Muchas gracias,*" I told him, while trying to say the U-turn was legal. I was so flustered it took me a long time to find my passport and my little *inglés-español* dictionary. A friendly couple inside the pizza place came outside and translated for me. They told me not to pay any cash to him and to challenge the ticket. After a few minutes and a slice of pizza, he gave me a warning and rode away.

Lynn told me later what this was and said I did the right thing.

"It's *la mordida,*" she said, translated literally as "the little bite." She said it's an attempt by *la policia* to shake down *turistas* for about $50. Everybody in Baja knows about it, and apparently many people pay it.

The English-language newspapers in Baja wrote about *la mordida* frequently, and the new Tijuana and Rosarito police chiefs issued statements pledging that they would put a stop to it. I learned later that it was illegal under Mexican law for a police officer to accept cash for a fine.[2] Apparently, however, *la policia* considered it part of their benefits package to supplement low wages.

Another Baja friend said that all of it was a dance between *la policia* and the driver, and I needed to learn how to dance. Harald, a German poet, said in 2009 it should be called "*el baile de la mordida.*"

First, people told me, be nice. Say something neutral, like "*Hola,*" then tell them "*no habla español,*" just as I did. Second, ask *la policia* to explain the traffic infraction *en*

---

[2] Survival Guide to the Mexican Legal System; Strickland, B.K.; International Gateway Insurance Brokers, Inc., Chula Vista, CA 91910; 1997; p. 24

inglés, because many have trouble doing this. Third, deny any wrongdoing and never agree to pay on the spot. Tell them to write the ticket and agree to follow them to *la comisaria*.

According to locals, this usually resulted in a verbal warning for two reasons. First, they explained, *la policia* didn't want to write a ticket and go to *la comisaria*, because they wouldn't get all the money for themselves. Second, the time they spent taking you to the station was time they could be using to shake down someone else. At least that was the locals' reasoning.

If you decided to avoid the hassle and pay *la mordida*, locals said to show them only a little of your money and tell them that's all you had. Otherwise, they would want more.

Since that first traffic stop, I've been through Tijuana and Rosarito many times, before and after I moved here. Most of the time, *la policia* didn't stop me at all. Other times, I've had the opportunity to practice my dancing.

They stopped me in Tijuana once to demand my Mexican insurance papers, which I showed them, and they let me go.

The accusation about not signaling a lane change was ridiculous—nobody in Baja does that. One of the two guys seemed curious about the Charger, which was becoming the official vehicle of the Mexican *federales*. I motioned for him to sit in the front passenger seat. After looking over the interior for a moment, he got out and rode away.

In 2008, Hugo Torres, the new mayor of Rosarito, tried to curtail *la mordida* and it seemed to diminish. He also created bilingual "mail-in" traffic tickets so people who knew they were guilty could accept a ticket and pay their fines by mail without having to go to *la comisaria*.

Before that, many expatriates had tales of *el baile de la mordida*. Eileen at Bajamar tells of paying $100 US after they threatened to take her cherished dog to the pound because the dog was riding in the front seat with her. A dog in the front seat is illegal because it might distract the driver, but dogs ride in the front seats in hundreds of vehicles in Baja. I've seen a Chihuahua nestling in the arms of one driver.

One of my favorite tales is from Joanna, who owns a small cafe and art gallery on Route 1 near Primo Tapia. *La policia* sit in front of their small *comisaria* on the mile-long Primo Tapia strip waiting to pounce on *Americano* drivers. They stopped her one evening, just after she closed the cafe for the day, and told her the taillights weren't working on the aging Mercedes with California license plates. One guy was standing next to her window, holding his flashlight next to his face and shining the bright light in her eyes so she couldn't see him.

She got out of the car and went to see the taillights for herself, joining a second guy who was standing back there. Both taillights were on. However, the guy said only part of the lights were working. She tried explaining to him that the other part of the taillights was for the brakes, but he insisted the light was *disperfecto*. He wanted $55 US and they started arguing.

The first one moved around to the passenger side of the car, still holding his flashlight next to his face. He opened the rear car door and her big red dog Mika snarled at him. The guy backed off and closed the door. Mika started barking at him and his flashlight.

Joanna threw a fit, told them she lived in Baja, owned the nearby cafe, and *la mordida* was hurting business.

"I only made $15 all day because *turistas* are fed up with stuff like this and don't come to Baja anymore," she shouted.

"Let her go," said the guy with the flashlight, still looking at Mika's snarling mouth. The other one was reluctant to give up. Joanna kept shouting and Mika kept barking, starting to attract a lot of attention. The guy with the flashlight said it again, more urgently this time: "Let her go." So they did. She says they don't like to deal with a crazy woman and a barking dog.

My closest call was during a brief visit in 2006 at the north end of Rosarito after buying cheaper Pemex gas on the way to the San Diego airport. I saw *el carro policia* sitting on the side of the street up ahead and I looked down at the speedometer to check my speed. Unfortunately, I missed seeing the *Alto* sign in the median and drove right past it.

He turned on the siren and lights and pulled alongside. I stopped and he leaned toward me. I was ready to negotiate and pay *la mordida*, partly because I was guilty and partly because I was in a hurry to return the rental car and catch a flight. However, he didn't give me the chance.

"Come with me," he said very clearly. There was no way out—he saw me go through the stop sign, he could speak good *inglés*, and he didn't try to get *la mordida*.

La comisaria was three miles or more away on the other end of town. He decided to use the nearby limited access highway rather than making a U-turn and going down the main street. With him in the lead, we became stuck behind a slow-moving old truck just before the right turn entrance.

That's when *el policia* made a huge mistake and passed the truck to turn onto the highway. I didn't have enough room to go around it before the truck also made the right hand turn.

Usually, I consider such situations are ethics tests— right versus wrong. I tell my three sons to choose right instead of wrong, always. However, that time, in a split second, I chose the left turn entrance leading to Tijuana, a short sprint up the toll road. I stepped on the gas and had that rental car up to the 70 mph speed limit in just a few heartbeats. It was a huge adrenaline rush.

I'm not bragging about making a high-speed getaway. I know it was wrong to run. I'm not proud of what I did, especially because I was guilty. So, I confessed to the whole family when I got back to Maryland, as a way of telling them never to do what I had done.

Friends in Baja told me later I was very fortunate *el policia* didn't chase me down and put me in jail. Worse yet, they said, he might have beat the stuffing out of me and then put me in jail.

Nevertheless, when I think about it now and then, I get a grin just imagining what *el policia* thought when he looked back and I was nowhere in sight.

I bet he thought he should have asked for *la mordida*.

In mid December 2007, I saw an article in the *Baja Times* newspaper warning *turistas* about carjackers in Baja, so I decided to drive the Charger back to Maryland at Christmas.

I would become "Americano Incognito" when I returned to Baja. My immigration agent Rosella would help me get a Mexican driver's license. I would buy her 1997 Dodge Caravan with Mexican license plates and register it in Baja.

A week later I was back in Maryland.

Chapter 3:
Driving in Mexico

When I returned to Baja in January 2008, neighbors in Plaza del Mar were astounded that I was able to get a Mexican driver's license, register my van, and get Mexican license plates all in one day.

"How did you do that?" they wanted to know. I said it was easy—Rosella did it for me, and they would laugh. But it was true.

Before I went back to Maryland for Christmas, Rosella obtained information from the Baja driver's license office so I could study and take the test when I returned. What she gave me was one piece of paper, 8 1/2 x 11, printed on both sides, so faded it looked like a third or fourth generation copy. I asked her for the booklet itself. She said that was the whole thing.

The paper had drawings of road signs on one side, such as stop signs, no U-turn, no left turn, etc., and the definition below each one. It wasn't much more than the one page at the back of the AAA TourBook for Mexico. On the other side, it had six or eight sample questions, with the answers. Both sides were *en español*, but even I could figure it out.

I recalled all the preparation Maryland required before people could take a test. When our three sons prepared for their written tests, they had to attend a formal driver education course for a couple of weeks each day after school and study a couple of books. However, that was Maryland. This was Mexico.

The other part of the preparation in Mexico was a physical exam, which Rosella arranged for me in December. It consisted of going to the *Cruz Roja* local office in Rosarito, around the corner from her mother's immigration service office. A young medic took my blood pressure and checked my pulse rate, measured my height in meters, weighed me in kilograms, asked my blood type, and checked the color of my hair and eyes against my Maryland driver's license.

He didn't understand hazel, the eye color on my Maryland driver's license, so he decided I had *ojos verde.* I never had green eyes before and it sounded cool. He signed the examination form and the front desk charged me eighty pesos.

When I returned in January, Rosella had prepared the six-page application, ready for the visit to the driver's license office. She had gone to the municipal building a couple of days before to talk with people and make sure the papers were in order.

She had informed the officials that I didn't read or speak *español,* so they would allow her to translate the questions for me. All I had to do was not say anything *en español.* We met at 8 a.m. at the municipal building when they opened, and we were first in line to take the test.

Rosella has a can-do attitude, a quick and easy laugh, and a great smile. She dresses the part of a professional businesswoman in attractive but no-nonsense high heels. She styles her hair differently on special days and applies just the right amount of makeup to accent her natural Latina good looks. In her mid thirties, she can still turn men's heads at twenty paces. When she's up close and touches your arm lightly to show her empathy, you want to do what she wants.

What she wanted that day was to obtain my driver's license in less than an hour, before she went to her mother's office for work.

The *hombres* at the driver's license office were simply no match for her determination. The *oficial* at the desk inspected each page of the application and verified the information by comparing it with my passport, Mexican resident visa, and Maryland driver's license. He stood me up against the wall to confirm my height in meters and compared that with the height on the medical examination paper from the *Cruz Roja*. Everything was fine until he checked the color of *los ojos*.

He didn't think they were *verde*. He and Rosella took turns putting their faces close to mine and looking at my eyes, negotiating the color. They agreed my eyes weren't blue or brown or black. He wasn't sure what color to call them. She touched him on his arm and he decided they really were *verde*.

Taking the actual written test was relatively easy and my friends laughed even more when I described it. It was on a touch-screen computer monitor, with the examiner watching to make sure Rosella didn't touch the screen for me. She read each question *en inglés*, I asked for clarification, and then I touched one of the three multiple-choice answers. I joked with her *en inglés* that it would be embarrassing if we failed the test.

I think there were ten questions, most of them on the one-page paper I got in December. Therefore, it wasn't hard. Most questions were about speed limits. A couple were about distances—how many meters away from the intersection do you have to park, etc. I missed only one, because neither of us knew the answer.

Then Rosella found the driving examiner and we all rode together to take the driving test in my Caravan. He was tall, a handsome *hombre* about Rosella's age, spoke very good *inglés*, and smiled a lot. He sat in the front passenger seat and Rosella sat behind me so he could talk with both of us easily. I could tell he liked Rosella because he talked to her a lot *en español* and he didn't pay much attention to my driving.

We drove around for maybe five minutes, turning left, turning right, stopping, backing up, making a U-turn, making a three-point turnaround, etc. Simple stuff; no parallel parking. We went back to the municipal building, he signed the form and handed it to Rosella, and then asked for her phone number so he could punch it into his cell phone.

After I posed for my digital picture, I received my license. It took another ten minutes to get the title and tags, walking from one window to another in the same room to pay here, present papers there, pay over there, etc. Compared to the motor vehicle office in Maryland, it was a model of efficiency. No taking numbers, no lines, only a few people waiting.

Rosella waved *adios* to me and drove away, headed for work. I put the tags on in the parking lot and thanked the parking attendant for lending me a screwdriver. The whole thing took less than an hour. It cost a total of only $140 for everything—driver's license, registration, title, and tags.

One interesting footnote: Mexican driver's licenses do not include hair color. However, they do include a lot of *informacion* on the back that might be helpful on licenses in the USA also. One thing is the blood type. Another thing is the name, address, and phone number of someone to contact in case of emergency.

My Mexican license says to contact Rosella, of course. Who else?

As in the USA, getting a driver's license in Mexico is just the beginning. People learn a lot more from experience than the test material covers, especially in Baja. I learned some valuable lessons, including:

Do not drive after dark if you can avoid it because the potholes and speed bumps are too hard to see. The son of Helanne, a Dutch writer, hit a huge pothole one night on the highway enroute to a restaurant. He lost control and his convertible flipped over, killing him.

There is usually a very good reason for speed limit signs where the road hugs the hills and has no shoulders. One good reason is that rocks of every size can come loose at any time and fall off the hill right in front of your car.

Obey the signs warning drivers to take precautions because the curve ahead is dangerous—*"Precaución, Curva Peligrosa."* Actually, I learned that the curve might not be as dangerous as what might be in the curve. One time I found a flatbed truck stalled in my lane in a tight curve, with the driver standing on the centerline pouring gasoline into the gas tank. Another time, I found a good-sized boulder.

The most valuable lesson I learned was the safest way to turn left in Baja when you meet oncoming traffic on a two-lane road. You're supposed to pull off the road on the right side, stop, and make certain nobody is behind you before turning left across the road. Some people say this is the law; others say it is just good common sense. Whatever…it's a fact of life.

Also, it is dangerous to use your turn signal to indicate you intend to turn left on a two-lane road. The reason is because Baja drivers usually tailgate, and they think you are signaling that it's okay for them to pass you on the left. So, they zoom around you.

Maybe the worst mistake you can make on a two-lane road is using the left turn signal and stopping in the road to wait for oncoming traffic to come past. I learned this from an accident right in front of the entrance to the Plaza del Mar club section—not my accident, luckily.

Friends of neighbors Scott and Lupé were turning left into the community and made this mistake. After the oncoming traffic cleared, the car approaching from behind them smashed into their left-turning car, injuring them and the other driver. Just like in the USA, serious accidents like this require drivers to stay at the scene until authorities investigate what happened.

I Love Baja!

Scott said authorities determined that the friends caused the accident, and they had to pay a fine of $500 US. He said the friends also had to pay the cost of repairing the other driver's car. Fortunately, authorities did not charge his friends with a criminal offense or put them in jail.

One of my fellow writers was not so fortunate. Authorities considered his auto accident a criminal offense, partly because it involved driving while intoxicated and partly because his car destroyed a utility pole. They arrested him and kept him in jail for five days in Rosarito until he paid more than $1,500 US in damages and fines. After they let him out of jail, authorities kept his car impounded as part of their investigation.

It was an awful experience, according to one friend who visited him in jail. He was in a cell with two others, sleeping on cardboard on the concrete floor, with only one blanket to keep him warm during the 45-degree December nights. The friend took water and food to him, with enough for his cellmates to share. The only toilet was a trough, and the stench was almost unbearable.

Jacki, an American poet, has a greater tale of woe involving an auto accident in Baja more than twenty years ago. She suffered a head concussion and couldn't remember the accident. The Mexican family in the other car said she crossed the centerline and hit them head on. Everybody survived. She had no Mexican liability insurance and had to live in a Mexican jail until she paid $10,000 US in cash for all the medical bills, car damages, and fines.

Doris and Walter, friends in Plaza del Mar, have an entertaining and informative story about Mexican auto insurance, with twists and turns and a happy ending. It also illustrates why foreigners driving in Mexico should buy auto liability insurance from a Mexican auto insurer.

They were heading south on the bypass between Tijuana and *Playas de Tijuana* one afternoon and Doris was driving. An aggressive driver in the northbound lanes bumped another car across the median strip and into their lane. It ricocheted off the rear of their car into other cars behind them and killed a motorcyclist. They weren't injured, but their rear wheel was damaged so much they couldn't drive their car.

Traffic accidents in Mexico with serious damages become a crime scene with a swarm of police investigators, especially when the accident involves personal injuries and fatalities. Mexican authorities detain everybody until they determine responsibility and resolve auto accident claims. Authorities do not recognize personal liability auto insurance from USA insurance companies, partly because of delays in accepting responsibility.

"They were on the scene lickety-split," says Doris, "telling us not to move and demanding to see our Mexican insurance papers. They were very concerned and courteous, trying out their best, but minimal, English. They paid no attention to our comprehensive auto insurance from a U.S. company for driving in Mexico. They wanted to see our Mexican-issued insurance, which we tried explaining was only liability."

Others involved in the accident translated for Doris and Walter, telling them to call their Mexican insurance company for help even if the company was only providing liability insurance and wasn't the more comprehensive insurance that would eventually cover the accident expenses. The Mexican insurance company sent an insurance adjuster to the scene to represent them, and insurance adjusters arrived for other drivers involved in the accident. Everybody headed to the police station.

"Our new best friend and volunteer interpreter, who actually was the boyfriend of the daughter whose mother had hit us, gave us a ride," says Doris. "After waiting almost two hours for the policeman to show up, we all crowded into one small room. It wasn't big enough for anybody except the drivers and the insurance adjusters, and, in my case, an interpreter. There wasn't room for Walter, never mind our dog. I was on my own."

A nondescript man walked into the room and sat down at a table in the front. Using a paper flip chart on an easel, a police officer began reconstructing the traffic accident. Suddenly, Doris realized the guy at the table was the judge, holding court and hearing the case right then. After several rounds of back and forth in *ingles* and *español* between the drivers and insurance representatives, everyone was satisfied with the accuracy of the drawing.

Mexican justice can be swift in such circumstances, with guilty parties going directly to jail until they pay all damages and fines. In cash, unless they have Mexican liability insurance. After hearing this particular case *en español*, the judge ruled that the aggressive hit-and-run driver caused the multiple-car accident. None of those present was at fault and they were free to go. The drivers would have to pay for their own damages and arrange repairs. And towing.

With the help of their volunteer interpreter, Doris and Walter arranged for the Mexican tow truck that had hauled their car from the accident scene to move the car from in front of the police station.

"The tow truck driver said he wasn't permitted to tow it into the USA, which everybody could see just across the border fence, about a mile north," says Doris. After negotiating a price, they decided to have the tow truck take the vehicle to their casa in Plaza del Mar, straight down the toll road, more than thirty miles south.

Once underway, they learned the tow truck driver also had to take the crushed motorcycle to a place in Tijuana. So they wound their way through downtown Tijuana on a Saturday night, dragging the damaged car behind, Doris and Walter crowding into the front seat with the driver, holding Sadie their Schnauzer on their laps. They dropped off the motorcycle wreckage and the driver took the back way out of town, up and across and down the Tijuana hills, heading past Rosarito for their place.

"I think the truck was from the thirties or forties," says Doris. "It could hardly make the hills and the windows wouldn't go up. We were freezing but the fresh air kept us from asphyxiating on the gasoline fumes."

"How far is it?" she says the tow truck driver kept asking.

"A little bit," Walter kept responding. "*Un poquito . . . diez kilometers!*" Doris thought the driver might abandon them along the road at any minute.

"The driver must never have been outside of Tijuana and had no idea where he was going or that he'd taken on such a long journey," she says. "We paid the guy a hefty bunch of cash, including a generous tip when we finally arrived at Plaza del Mar, and he drove away happy."

Of course, then they had to get their car back across the border for repairs. They learned the next day there are some American towing companies with contracts to move vehicles across the border. On Monday a big, new shiny diesel flatbed arrived to take their SUV back to the U.S.

After listening to Jacki's story and hearing what happened with the other writer, I resolved to be more careful than usual with my driving in Baja.

After listening to Doris tell her story, I had Rosella double-check to see if my Mexican liability insurance policy covers everything I need.

I think it does. I hope so.

I Love Baja!

Chapter 4:
Piensa Verde – Think Green

During the January 2008 rainy season, chilly rain blew against the windows and under the door of my little apartment in Plaza del Mar.

Rain is a big deal in northern Baja and in San Diego, where the normal annual rainfall is less than ten inches, most of it in winter. San Diego news media warn people days in advance of oncoming winter rainstorms, encouraging residents to stock up on supplies and sandbags. It is much like the U.S. East Coast preparing for hurricanes. Cities and towns in northern Baja are especially vulnerable because they don't have much underground drainage infrastructure. Baja newspapers print maps showing areas with a historical risk of flooding.

Daytime January temperatures are usually in the sixties. Nighttime temperatures are sometimes only forty five —more than twice as warm as back in Maryland—however Baja houses don't have central heat. I bundled up to stay warm. The apartment had a radiator-style electric heater, like the one I had in the cabin on my old boat on the Chesapeake; it kept me warm as long as I was within a few feet. However, it was useless as a room heater. I started wearing a kerchief cap and a hooded pullover to sleep. I still caught a cold, developed bronchial pneumonia, and had to get antibiotics from a *clinica* in La Misión.

One morning after the fog lifted, I was surprised to see white stuff on the steps from my balcony to the street. I thought for a moment it was the remnants of frost. But it was just evaporated salt residue, blown all the way up to my little apartment by the stiff wind from the ocean 100 yards downhill.

For some reason, electricity is also unreliable in Baja (locals call it *la luz*—the light). I was accustomed to frequent electrical outages back in Maryland, especially during winter ice storms or summer thunderstorms, so a few hours in Baja without *luz* didn't cause me to panic. However, forty five degrees is chilly no matter where you are, especially without a little electric heater. That's why some people in Baja have one-room heaters that burn bottles of propane.

Water is a bigger deal in Baja, with a desert climate and landscape, and not enough ground water to meet the growing demands of homes and businesses. I learned that the city water supply was not reliable in many communities.

In Plaza del Mar, for example, the water from the faucet or the shower was only a trickle on some days. When the water started to trickle, people began preparing for the worst. They knew it might take days for the city water to begin flowing again. The first step was to *piensa verde* and conserve. Stop baths and delay showers. Let the dirty dishes and the dirty laundry pile up a few days. If it's brown, flush it down; if it's yellow, let it mellow, as the green mantra states.

Usually, city water in the La Misión area began flowing again after a couple of days. One time, however, the water was off for more than a week. Dozens of local residents signed a petition demanding officials in Rosarito and Ensenada take action. Three days later, city water was flowing again. It may have been unrelated to the petitions.

Nobody could ever explain to my satisfaction why the city water stopped flowing frequently, or who was responsible. Some old-timers blamed newly arrived expatriates trying to grow green grass lawns in a desert rather than planting natural succulents. A few oceanfront lawns in filmmaker Dino de Laurentis' neighborhood of Punta Piedra (Point of Stone) are big enough for croquet courts. Other long time residents say the La Misión area suffers because it's on the outer city limits of Rosarito and Ensenada. They say water officials conserve water for businesses and homes in higher population areas of both cities.

What? The image of some bureaucrat sending a city water worker out every few days to shut off a big valve somewhere seemed comical. "Hey José," I could imagine the official saying, "The downtown water pressure is getting low —go shut off the water on the edge of town." Neither explanation seemed like the whole reason. Another explanation was that water officials had to shut off the water now and then to repair the aging infrastructure and install new water pipes while widening Route 1. Maybe it was all of these, and more.

In the summer of 2008, the *Baja News* tabloid had a front-page article[3] reporting that some communities on the Baja Gold Coast had received notice of water cutbacks. However, the article didn't explain who ordered the cutbacks, or why, or when, or how often they would occur. The same article also reported that Mexico had a new law requiring all new developments to build desalination plants to supply their own water needs, especially for golf courses.

My neighbor Tim educated me about a storage tank called a pila, which many Mexicans homes and businesses have. Black plastic pilas are everywhere, many sitting atop short wooden towers low enough for a water tanker truck to fill the pilas and high enough for gravity to empty them. Local roadside hardware stores sell smaller pilas for homes.

---

[3] "Baja News," July 24, 2008

Home Depot sells bigger ones with pumps and plumbing so expatriates can bury them underground out of sight. Some underground pilas are concrete, big enough to hold an entire tanker truck of water. Usually tanker trucks get the water from wells, and the water may have high salt content and other impurities. It's good enough for everything except drinking and cooking, but some expats say it leaves a white film in the dishwasher. Pilas are very sensible, the same concept as the water storage tank my sister Sherry and her husband Doug had when they lived in the Idaho mountains.

The Club section of Plaza del Mar has huge community pilas buried alongside the street and connected to the city water supply, each big enough to supply several homes and condo units. City water goes into the pila, normally, keeping it full and in ready reserve. When city water stops, a float switch signals the pump to start supplying water to homes. The trickle of water is because the pump pressure is not as strong as the city water pressure. Pilas in other sections in Plaza del Mar and in some other communities in the La Misión area don't work as well. When that happens, people scramble to find friends with toilets and showers.

The Plaza del Mar homeowner association was responsible for checking water levels in the pilas, but Tim didn't trust anyone. He was the de facto first responder, because he was a handyman for hire and took care of several properties. At the first sign of a trickle, he was out there on top of the pilas, checking the water level, giving frequent updates, and urging the HOA representatives to call the water truck people and place orders for tanker trucks to fill the pilas if it came to that. He remembered hauling water from the swimming pool to help people flush their toilets during one shortage and he didn't want to do that again.

Originally, the HOA was supposed to pay to have water trucks fill the pilas if city water stopped. However, the HOA announced in 2008 that it would pay for only one refill per year. Residents had to pay for any more than that, at about $25 per truckload. In late 2009, the HOA decided to quit paying for the first truckload of water.

Eventually, I devised my own backup for the pila alongside the street in case of a real water emergency coupled with loss of electricity to the pila pump. A few plastic twenty-litre jugs of *agua purificada* hold enough for a few days until the emergency passes. It cost less than a dollar to fill each jug. Sure enough, I had to break into my backup supply one time.

It happened after I awoke to find no water one morning. My next-door neighbors and I checked the pila. It was so low the pump was sucking air rather than water. The pump motor was overheating and had that smell of an impending electrical fire. Jody called her husband Pete, who was back in the states for a few days, and he said to shut off the motor. I didn't see a cutoff switch, but farm boys know a thing or two about electricity. I asked Jody for a screwdriver. I just loosened the electrical plate, inserted the screwdriver, and shorted out the circuit.

We saved the motor, a truck refilled the pila, a handyman replaced the electrical faceplate, and somebody found and reset the circuit breaker. The pump started pumping and water started flowing again.

I Love Baja!

Chapter 5:
Popotla Fishing Village

The tiny fishing village of Popotla (poh-pōt'-lah) offers a unique opportunity to buy fresh *mariscos* directly from local fishermen. It was the destination of my first Baja mini-roadtrip in January 2008, and Tim was my tour guide.

Popotla has one of the few coves on the Pacific Ocean of northern Baja with vehicle access to a shallow sloping beach and no rocks. As a result, *pescadores* can use pickups or 4x4 vehicles with trailers to launch their twenty-foot open fishing *pangas,* beach the boats after fishing, load them back onto boat trailers, and drive away.

The village is located on Route 1 a few miles south of downtown Rosarito, adjacent to Foxploration Movie Studios. You can't miss it, although no highway signs mark the fishing village. People just turn onto the dirt road at the big white sculpture that marks the southern boundary of the Fox property and head toward the ocean and the buildings in the distance.

It was low tide when we arrived just past noon and most of the fishermen had already returned from the ocean and sold the morning catch. Another boat was landing on the beach and two others were coming toward *la playa.*

Customers walk past the waiting albatrosses to meet the incoming two-person boats. They crowd around the sides of the boat, select what they wanted, negotiate *el precio,* and pay on the spot. The place was busy – maybe 100 people – but it wasn't crowded. Tim said the place would be packed *el domingo.*

There appear to be three basic categories of customers at Popotla. The first group is individuals who buy only a small amount for personal consumption. Vendors comprise the second group, buying a bucket or two and hoping to sell to customers who showed up after the boats arrived. They set up shop on tables, sometimes with a beach umbrella shading the catch as customers crowded around.

Fishmonger at Popotla Fishing Village

One vendor featured shrimp and raw *ostiones,* shucking the oysters and handing them to customers standing around the table. Customers could choose from a dozen different bottles of hot sauces to add a few drops of zest and then slurp the oysters from the shells into their mouths. It reminded me of living in Louisiana in the late 1960s.

Buyers for restaurants up the hill comprise the third group, buying fish, oysters, and lobsters, separating them into five-gallon buckets left over from construction projects. They lug the buckets up the sandy lane leading from the beach to the restaurants.

A short road between two rows of buildings halfway up the hill forms an intersection with the main road and creates a center for a makeshift marketplace. Street vendors hawk their wares that includes silver and jade jewelry, straw *sombreros* and sunglasses, shell bracelets and necklaces, and various trinkets.

On the edge of the cliff at the top of the hill, the road is narrower. Parked vehicles line both sides of the street. One-story little restaurants are primarily on the ocean side; shops with merchandise are primarily on the inland side. About two dozen small restaurants are jammed side-by-side along the cliff, offering space for eating while overlooking the ocean. One offered silver jewelry alongside a sample of the day's catch laid out on the counter—Red Snapper, Sea Bass, Bonita, etc.

Restaurant owners stand in the narrow road and try to entice drivers to stop and eat. Parking is scarce. Tim made a deal with an owner for free parking right in front in exchange for eating at his place, plus an appetizer of boiled *camarones*. The owner moved a parking cone to make space and directed my parallel parking effort.

A cooler of fresh *pescado* was at the restaurant entrance, along with buckets of *ostiones* and crabs. *Mas cangrejos* lay in rows on a work area near the kitchen. At the gas range, the cook was dropping three-quarter pound *langosta*s into hot oil in a round metal pan that was at least twenty four inches in diameter.

Customers who ordered fish could watch the entire cleaning and cooking process. I'm a retired fish griller and I stopped to watch. The fish cleaner took a fish from the cooler and prepared a butterfly filet of the whole fish. He slathered sauce onto the inside of the butterfly, put two whole fish sauce-side-up into a skinny iron basket, clamped the basket shut, and made *pescado a la parilla* over a charcoal fire in half a metal barrel. After a short time, the cook turned the basket over, the sauce dripped onto the hot charcoal, and smoke filled the air until the fish was done. It smelled *fantástico*.

I passed up the fish - probably a mistake - but we were there for a light lunch. The long, narrow room overlooking the ocean had plastic tables and plastic chairs advertising Tecate beer. A two-man band by the kitchen played and sang Mexican songs loudly. We split a dozen fresh oysters, followed by *tostados de camarones*. Tortilla chips, salsa, and hot sauces rounded out the meal. As we were leaving, the waiter walked past us carrying a platter with a mound of at least six California spiny lobsters split open and fresh from the charcoal grill.

Lobsters were a little pricey on the menu, but right off the boats, they were as low as 200 pesos for four lobsters weighing two kilos (4.4 pounds). At the exchange rate of 11 pesos to 1 dollar, that was less than $5 a pound for lobsters that were in the ocean a few hours earlier. I made a mental note to come back for lobster.

About a month later, the gang wanted some fresh lobster for a cookout. Tim, Georgiann, and I headed up to Popotla. The plan was to steam the lobsters for dinner and use the bodies to make lobster bisque for the next night. We sat on the restaurant deck in the late morning sun, snacking on salsa and chips, watching *pangas* bob on the ocean swells.

Tim said the price would be higher than my first trip, because it was later in the season, but he had a strategy. His plan was brilliant and simple—show them a Mexican 500-peso bill, worth about $45 at the time, and let the bidding begin. He headed down the sandy trail to the cove in his cutoffs and construction boots with the 500-peso bill in his hand, ready to show them the money.

Tim likes to look at a lobster's eyes and poke it see if it is still alive and kicking—kickers, he calls them. You want kickers because the others are dead, he says, and they release a toxin into their tail meat just before they die. He says most people don't know about this and fail to buy live ones. He also insists on no "shorts," the ones too small to be legal in the states.

His criteria drove up the price. However, he was able to get almost three kilos of kickers (2.2 pounds per kilo) for our 500 pesos. I think that means we paid about $7.50 US per pound for more than six pounds of lobster. My kilo math isn't perfect and I could be wrong.

The kickers were nice sized. He estimated one was seven or eight years old. They were great.

I've been back to Popotla many times since then, usually to share the experience with a few friends or visitors who have never been there. People always like it.

In late summer of 2009, I took my neighbors Leslie and her daughter Amanda, who lived in the Pyramid section of Plaza del Mar. Amanda was heading back to the states after a year in Baja writing songs and practicing vocals. Jack, a neighbor in the Arcos section, went with us so we would have somebody fluent *en español* to negotiate prices. He teaches English at the University in Ensenada, is a writer and a singer/songwriter/guitar player, and usually buys fresh seafood at *el Mercado de Mariscos* in Ensenada.

We parked on the main road near the oceanfront road and hiked to the cove to hunt for bargain seafood before choosing a place for Amanda's going-away lunch. She was enthralled by the juvenile Silky Sharks lying in a row, each one about thirty inches long. Jack negotiated to buy one for fifty pesos—only $3.85 US. The fishmonger expertly cut it into two long filets, and three bright yellow shark eggs plopped out onto the table. I asked him to bag *los huevos* and the shark eyeballs separately so we could take them too.

Back on restaurant row, we chose a little place with oceanfront tables and negotiated for a free crab appetizer sauteed in butter and garlic. For the entree, we ordered one of those whole fish, cut open into a butterfly, wrapped in aluminum foil with garlic sauce and herbs, and grilled over an open fire.

We sat in the midday sun, watching seagulls and pelicans and the crashing surf, enjoying the good life in Baja. The whole meal for four of us, including homemade taco chips and fresh *pico de gallo*, warm soft corn tortillas, plus beer and sodas, was 400 pesos including tip—about $30 US. Moreover, we had enough left over for another small meal.

As a favor, the cook used the shark eggs to make *huevos estrellados* for us. They turned out overcooked and almost tasteless, despite smearing them with the herb and garlic sauce from the grilled fish. Adventuresome Amanda also tried a shark eyeball. The rest of us were content to watch. I asked her later to describe the experience.

"I knew there was a hard white ball in the middle to remove, so I squeezed that out and ate the squishy part surrounding it," she said in an email. "It tasted like a soft, jellylike piece of fat. It was a fun experience in itself, but the best part was watching the reactions at the table as I did it."

Maybe she can work it into a blues song someday —*"Don't Think You Can Cheat, 'Cause You Know What I Eat."* Or something like that.

Amanda said later the fresh shark fillets were great and they fed her and her mother for several days. In addition, Jack said he found the recipe for the herb and garlic sauce in a Mexican cookbook, ready for a cookout at his *casa*, maybe with seared fresh tuna from Ensenada.

A couple of weeks later, I told some other people about the Popotla experience with Amanda, Leslie, and Jack. Right away, they wanted to make the trip and started planning a dinner at John and Mary Beth's place in La Misión, where Jack could demonstrate his grilling skills. However, Leslie, Ruth, John, Mary Beth, and Jack had conflicting schedules and we had to choose a date a week or more in the future.

The success of that trip and cookout led to another Popotla venture. Sandy had never been so she, Fritz, Fred,

Idalia, and I made the trip together. On the way back, we enjoyed tacos in Primo Tapia for lunch, and I showed them the way to the local *carniceria* and *panaderia.* Debbie, Annelise, and Vickie joined us for dinner, along with new neighbors Linda and Larry.

Both those trips and cookouts provided *delicioso* meals consisting of grilled *camarones,* halibut, Yellowtail *atun,* a local white fish that Idalia fried whole, and *ceviché mariscos* made fresh in front of us and served as an appetizer on a *tostado.*

Popotla—it's worth the trip, in more ways than one.

I Love Baja!

Chapter 6:
Papá Swims with the Whales

My first Baja roadtrip of more than a few hours was a whale-watching expedition three months after I arrived in Baja. It was special because it gave me my first real insights into Mexican family life. The three-day experience with *trés* Mexican *mujeres* and their *niños* was something I'll never forget.

I had decided in December to see *las ballenas gris* in the spring at Scammon's Lagoon near *Guerrero Negro*, a town about halfway down the Baja peninsula. It's just south of the state line between *Baja California* and *Baja California Sur*. The tour book I received at my retirement party recommended Malarrimo Eco-Tours for whale watching. I asked Rosella what kind of documents I would need. She said I should take my U.S. passport, driver's license, and my Mexican resident immigrant visa. Also, I needed to make sure my Mexican auto insurance policy was valid in the southern state because most policies are just for the state where people live.

Rosella's *madre*, Alicia, said I might also need an interpreter because most Mexicans spoke only *español* south of Ensenada. She suggested Rosella. The last time Rosella had a real vacation trip was when she was nine years old, and her two kids had never been on a vacation trip. Her mother also suggested that I take her office assistant Triny, who lived with her mother and had never traveled anywhere.

I was going anyway and there would be room in the seven-passenger Caravan I bought from Rosella, so I agreed to take everybody. Rosella chose the weekend of February 2-4, because 5 *febrero* was *Dia de Constitución,* a Mexican national holiday. The kids would not miss school, and Rosella and Triny would not miss work. I would provide transportation and gas and pay Rosella as an interpreter. We would share costs for food, lodging, and the tickets for the whale watching tour.

While reading travel experiences on the Internet, I learned the road was only two narrow lanes most of the way, with many trucks and campers. I bought new local Baja maps to complement the AAA road map. Some people in Baja told me it would take about eight and a half hours for the 400 miles. However, Ellen and Rick from Bajamar told me the trip might take ten hours from Rosarito to Guerrero Negro because the road had hills and sharp curves through the mountains. They suggested stopping in Cataviña Saturday night, then driving three and a half hours on Sunday morning and going on the 11 a.m. whale tour. I reserved two double rooms in Cataviña—one for Rosella, her two kids, and Triny; another for me.

About the third week of January, Rosella said she wanted to invite Alejandra, a close friend from Ensenada, who wanted to scatter her father's ashes in the lagoon with the whales. Neither Alejandra nor her daughter had been on a trip like this, so why not? This filled all seven seats in my van. I ordered two more whale tour tickets online from Malarrimo. Rosella said not to bother reserving another motel room.

I wanted to have dinner at the Malarrimo restaurant in Guerrero Negro after the whale tour, because people who had been there recommended it as one of the best seafood restaurants on the Baja peninsula. However, I thought it might be too expensive for everyone else. Rosella said *no hay problema.* She and Alejandra would make food to take so we would not have to buy any meals on the road and we could save enough money to eat at the restaurant.

They wanted to cook and prepare everything at Alejandra's house in Ensenada on Friday evening, stay over, and leave on Saturday morning. Fine with me. I went to Rosarito on Friday afternoon to get Rosella, her two kids, and Triny after work. They limited their luggage to one bag each. However, they had several shopping bags of other stuff— snacks, games, books, toys, shoes, jackets for the boat ride, etc. We got all of it into the Caravan behind the third row of seats just before it started to rain.

Just when I thought we were ready to leave, Rosella said we had to stop and pick up her mother and take her to Ensenada because she was going there for the weekend. She still had some laundry to do and would have to take it with her. We loaded two laundry baskets into the remaining space between the front and second rows of seats. To keep us safe, Rosella hung the rosary from her daughter's confirmation on the rear-view mirror over the dash. We were off.

We made it to Alejandra's house in Ensenada about 6:30 p.m. and she arrived shortly with groceries. She squeezed my van into her locked garage for the night and started making food. They made a quick meal that was *ensalada,* plus flour tortillas wrapped around a mixture of *carne asada, chile,* and *frijoles.* We had plenty of food, fresh-ground *café,* and *agua en botella.*

I learned that Triny was twenty one with a high school degree, *sin novio,* and living at home rent-free with her mother. Rosella was thirty four, a year short of finishing high school, with an eleven-year-old daughter and four-year-old son. She had separated recently from her husband in Ensenada and was living in a small rental house in Rosarito owned by her mother. Alejandra was in her late thirties, divorced, with a seven year-old daughter and nineteen-year-old son out on his own.

Los trés niños played upstairs. I sat at the table sipping *café*, asking now and then how to say something *en español*, and watching them make the food. They prepared food to store in the refrigerator overnight—chicken with rice, pasta with tuna, chicken with lettuce salad, and more of the same tortillas we had for dinner. Bedtime was simple. I slept on a futon over by the wall and everyone else slept in the two bedrooms upstairs—kids in one room, women in the other. One *baño* was upstairs and one was downstairs.

Desayuno the next morning was tortillas *con huevos*. They cooked another *pollo* for the trip, made more food, and made fresh coffee. We collected more luggage and shopping bags from Alejandra's house. They packed the rear of the Caravan full and Rosella took the wheel with Alejandra as copilot and navigator. All of them recited a Spanish traveler's *oración* and we drove away before 10 a.m. They gave me the captain's seat behind Rosella; Triny took the one behind Alejandra and all three kids snuggled into the third row. Rosella tuned into a local Spanish radio station and began singing along.

About ten minutes later, Alejandra's daughter shouted "*¡Papá, Papá!*" Alejandra told Rosella to stop. They spoke in animated Spanish for a few moments and I could tell something was wrong. Rosella explained to me that Alejandra had forgotten to bring her father's ashes. Her father always said he had dreams about swimming with the whales, but he never was able to make the trip to see them. Alejandra wanted to make the journey to actualize his dreams.

Back to her house we went. His ashes were in a varnished little wooden box, which Alejandra's daughter clutched tightly for a long time before giving it back to her mother for safekeeping. I wasn't sure if the daughter had known Alejandra's father. Apparently she knew the significance of this trip.

Back on Route 1 we rolled over the hills, down into valleys between the mountains, along fields of cacti, and past the Santo Tomas and L.A. Cetto vineyards. We wound our way from Colonet to Camalu and into San Quintin, past acres of agriculture hothouses and vast fields growing Driscoll strawberries for sale in the USA. Soon, the highway was closer to the ocean and we drove past miles of oceanfront land without a structure in sight, actual sand dunes rather than cliffs, with nice breakers. A new seaside development appeared in the distance. Bright colored flags at the sales office fluttered in the ocean breeze.

We drove up and away from the coastline into the mountains and headed for Cataviña. Near El Rosario, we had to stop and get out of the van at a military checkpoint for drugs. *No hay problema.* We were going south and drug traffickers go north.

The road had more twists and turns and required slower speeds. At a tight left turn on a downhill grade we saw an overturned truck and trailer rig on our side of the road, clinging to the steep hillside with its wheels pointed back to the road. There were dozens of campers and RVs and we had to poke along behind a convoy of several at one point.

Rocas gigante filled the landscape; piles of rocks, hills of rocks. We stopped to take pictures beside thirty-foot tall cacti and let *los niños* climb on *las rocas.* We arrived in Cataviña about 4 p.m., with time to unload and get into the two rooms before the early darkness.

Nights in the high desert are clear and cold, yet I didn't see any sign of heat in the rooms. The hot water was warmish and that was good enough. However, there weren't enough towels for the seven of us. Maybe they had toilet paper somewhere. I couldn't find it in my room. Fortunately, people in Baja learned long ago to carry toilet paper on journeys.

Rosella and Alejandra took charge of organizing the overnight stay, consolidating all the food and supplies into one room with two double beds. That would be my room.

All six of them planned to sleep in the other room with two double beds. It didn't seem logical to me to leave one double bed empty in my room while three women and three kids tried to sleep on two beds in the other room. Rosella explained that it would be inappropriate for Triny to stay with me in my room while she and Alejandra and their kids stayed in the other room. She also said it would be unwise for her and her son to sleep in the extra bed in my room because her son or daughter might say something about it to her jealous separated husband. She hadn't told him about the trip.

Just before bedtime, I resolved to sleep in the van and give my room to them. I bundled up with an extra layer of clothing under my winter coat, knocked on their door, and called for Rosella. When she came to the door, I handed her the key to my room and said I was going to stay in the van.

"No, no, no, Mr. Miller," she said. "We can't let you do that."

She wouldn't take the key and she shut the door. I went back to my room. Fifteen minutes later, I heard a knock on my door. The *trés mujeres* had talked it over and worked out a compromise. Triny and Alejandra would sleep in the extra bed in my room. Rosella would sleep in the other room with her four-year-old son in one bed. Her eleven-year-old daughter and Alejandra's daughter would share the other bed.

I awoke about 4 o'clock in the morning with a nagging feeling that something was wrong with our reservations at Malarrimo Eco-Tours. I couldn't get back to sleep and I went to sit in the lobby and review the plans. I got the map from the van and looked it several times. Finally, I realized that Guerrero Negro was in the Mountain Standard time zone. That meant we might be an hour late unless we left Cataviña an hour earlier than we planned. I couldn't believe it—the only solution was to awaken everyone early. Afraid I wouldn't wake up on time if I went back to bed, I stayed in the lobby and drifted in and out of sleep.

I asked the desk clerk to wake me at 5 o'clock and I knocked on Rosella's room door to tell her we had to leave early. I wasn't sure what kind of reaction to expect; maybe she was not a morning person. She gave me a perplexed look and then quickly organized the early departure with Alejandra and Triny.

We let *los niños* sleep while we packed everything back into the van. We carried them outside still in their pajamas, wrapped in blankets, and were on the road by 6 a.m. The sun was coming up over the mountains and we were on time. We sped along the deserted highway in the early morning, making good time, listening to CDs, and looking forward to seeing the whales.

I still couldn't shake the feeling something else might be wrong. I kept looking at the map every now and then. About an hour before Guerrero Negro, Rosella asked me if I knew how to get to the tour operator place. Suddenly I realized I didn't know anything about the location. I said the town was pretty small and we would find it.

The little tour book had a telephone number for Malarrimo. We couldn't get a cell phone signal. I looked at the map again and found the word Malarrimo right there on the map, plain as could be. Unfortunately, the word was almost a half inch from the words Guerrero Negro, maybe fifteen miles farther, on a smaller road. If that's where the tour began, we might miss our 11 a.m. departure although we left Cataviña an hour early.

My stomach was churning and I was stressing when we came to the turnoff for Guerrero Negro. Suddenly, there was a huge highway sign saying Malarrimo Eco-Tours was only a few hundred yards away. I can't remember when I've been so relieved.

A shuttle bus drove us about twenty minutes to the departure point, probably where the word Malarrimo was on the map. They assigned us to a twenty three-foot *panga* with a tour guide and a cooler with drinks and food. We strapped life jackets over our coats and I pulled the hood of my offshore rain gear over my head to protect against the chilly wind.

The boat eased away from the gangplank into the lagoon and crashed through the choppy water, sending salt spray over us frequently during the thirty minute ride. We slowed and the tour guide talked by two-way radio with tour guides in other boats looking for whales. When one tour guide spotted whales, the boats would race to that spot. We saw several whales and took pictures, but none came close enough to our boat for us to touch. After ninety minutes or so, all the boats moved closer together for a lunch break, bobbing up and down on the swells.

Whale Petting at Scammon's Lagoon – Photo by Ruben Mireles

After lunch, Alejandra told the tour guide what she wanted to do. He eased our boat about fifty yards away from the others and shut down the outboard motor. We drifted quietly while Alejandra took the varnished wooden box from a plastic bag and opened it. She and her daughter began sprinkling the ashes on the water and said a little prayer. Rosella took some pictures.

The tender moment lasted only a minute or two. We watched silently as the ashes floated on the sparkling surface of the blue lagoon in the afternoon sun.

Papá was swimming with the whales.

We saw several more whales during the afternoon. Some breached as close as fifteen feet from our *panga*. It was a great experience, a trip of a lifetime for all of us.

The boat trip lasted another hour or so and we were back at the motel before 4 p.m. Nobody discussed the room arrangements this time—we had bonded, like *familia*, and Alejandra and Triny shared the upstairs room with me. Exhausted, we showered and took naps until *la cena* at Malarrimo. The food was as good as people said it would be, and we celebrated the occasion with the house specialty of scallops fresh from the lagoon. The total tab for all seven of us, including a generous *propina*, was only 1,000 pesos, about $87 US at the time.

Trés Mujeres y Trés Niños after Watching Whales

We ate *desayuno* and *comida* out of the cooler the next day, made it to Ensenada just after dusk, and we were back to Rosarito before 8 p.m. I rested all the next day.

Rosella said later that Alejandra's daughter described the adventure to schoolmates as throwing her *abuelito* into the ocean. She said Alejandra had a new name for me—San Miguel.

She also said Paola Nicole asked her why I had tears in my eyes as I watched *Papá's* ashes floating on the water.

"I told her maybe it was the wind," she said with a little smile.

I grinned back at her, because both of us knew it wasn't the wind.

Chapter 7:

Puerto Nuevo Lobster Village

The lobster village of Puerto Nuevo is famous throughout Baja and in some parts of the USA. It's a small place dedicated almost exclusively to *langosta*, at exit Km49 on the Tijuana-Ensenada scenic toll road, maybe ten minutes south of the main part of Rosarito.

Beyond the archway at the main entrance on Route 1, the village has two main streets, about three blocks long, leading to and from the ocean cliffs. It has about three dozen lobster restaurants squeezed side-by-side on the three side streets between the two main streets.

It seems as if half the buildings in town are restaurants specializing in lobsters. Clothing and souvenirs hang in open shops and spill over into almost empty space along the sidewalks. It has the feel of a bustling open-air bazaar, particularly on weekends. You can buy regular food at a few other places in town, however most people head for the lobster restaurants.

People in southern California, as far away as Los Angeles, drive down for lobster and the Baja experience. PuertoNuevoLobster.com says the village has been a phenomenon since 1956, when local women started cooking lobsters in bubbling lard and selling them to outsiders.

Before the number of *turistas* declined, it served almost 700,000 lobsters a year Puerto Nuevo style. You can choose steamed or broiled if you don't like lard. Everybody says it's the place to go if you want *langostas* right out of the Pacific Ocean.

One weekend in October the main street shuts down for the annual lobster festival. Mexican beer companies and Baja wineries offer samples. Restaurants compete for top billing, and waiters compete for prizes while running through the village carrying trays with three glasses and a bottle of wine. A $15 ticket buys a *langosta* dinner, three small drinks, music, and watching traditional Mexican folklore dancers.

Madre y Niño at Puerto Nuevo Lobster Festival

Las *langostas* at Puerto Nuevo are not the ones with big claws, as in Maine or other famous lobster locales. These are California spiny lobsters, native to the cold Pacific waters from Monterrey, California, to the southern tip of the Baja peninsula. They have long antennae that protrude from their heads and sharp spines cover their bodies. That's how they got their name. Males can live up to thirty years, according to the California Department of Fish and Game, and can grow to over one meter, with some recorded catches of twenty-six pounds by divers.

The demand used to be so great most *langostas* caught locally and served in Puerto Nuevo restaurants were only five years old and barely legal size. They had to get larger lobsters from southern Baja and ship in frozen *langostas* from Cancun when fresh Baja *langostas* were out of season.

The legal size is anything more than three and one quarter inches, measured from the rear edge of the eye sockets to the rear edge of the body. Lobstermen call undersized *langostas* "shorts" if the body is shorter than that. Regulations require lobstermen to measure a *langosta* as soon as they pull it from the water. Generally, they are very careful about this. The penalty for getting caught with shorts, or possessing more than the allowed daily catch, can be severe—taking the catch, imposing a stiff fine, and impounding the boat.

Baja California issues licenses and enforces the season, which runs from mid-September through mid-February. It's illegal for restaurants to serve undersize *langostas*, also sometimes called "slippers." Government agents stroll the streets frequently and pop into restaurants periodically to keep the business legal.

Outside each restaurant at least one or two *hombres* shout at the passing cars, trying to attract people to stop and eat at that particular restaurant. You can negotiate the price of dinner through the car window—usually starting at about $15 for a meal with one-pounder. Depending on the time of day and amount of traffic, you might negotiate to get two smaller ones for $20 or less. During the early afternoon, after lunch and before dinner time, it's fun to just cruise along a couple of streets listening to the sales pitches, before you come back and commit to your favorite restaurant.

After agreeing on the price, the street hawker helps you find a place to park and leads you back to a restaurant. If you walk in without negotiating a price, a waiter usually brings a tray with three different sizes and you negotiate at your table. After you choose a "kicker" from the tray, you still have no guarantee that's the one they cook for you unless you watch the waiter take it to the kitchen. Otherwise, the cook simply grabs a lobster from the kitchen cold storage room.

The cook cuts it open lengthwise without separating the tail from the body, washes out the goop, and tosses it into the hot oil. Then she arranges the two halves on a platter with *frioles y arroz* and gives it to the waiter. When the waiter sets it on your table with some hot flour tortillas, it looks like you are getting *mucho mas* than you are. After diners finish eating, the kitchen staff picks the remaining bits of meat from the body to make *burritos langostas* for others. Locals told me to take all the leftovers home and make my own burritos.

I know that deep frying *langostas* takes care of a lot of bad things like bacteria. Despite what Tim says about always insisting on kickers, it probably doesn't matter that much whether the lobsters have been dead for an hour or so. Nevertheless, it's my money, and I'm paying for fresh *langosta*. More importantly, it's my tummy.

If you don't want to risk causing a scene in the restaurant by walking the waiter and your kickers to the kitchen, there is another way to increase your chances of getting live lobsters in Puerto Nuevo. You need to find a reputable family-run restaurant and become acquainted with the owner well enough to develop a trust with him or her. They are usually the ones standing at the cash register, while spouses and daughters prepare the food. The waiters are usually sons or daughters, and the street hawkers are mostly other family members—maybe nephews.

Tim and a couple of other friends I know had developed this trust, and I eat *langostas* only at the places they recommended. It's really no different than getting to know and trust a restaurant back in the states. The other way is to buy kickers, keep them iced down, and cook them at home.

When restaurant prices started to rise in response to supply and demand, Tim liked to buy a few kickers from one of the street hawkers with whom he had developed a trust. We tried this toward the very end of the season in February, when a short supply drove up the prices.

I put up $60 in cash and Tim made the deal with a street hawker to buy *seis* kickers, more than a pound apiece, for $10 each. We would come back the next afternoon, drop them into my little red cooler, and have lobsters with neighbors back in Plaza del Mar. I called Tim from Rosarito the next day and said I was running late. I planned to stop and pick up the lobsters on the way home rather than driving all the way to Plaza del Mar to get him, then driving back to Puerto Nuevo. I spotted his contact so I rolled right up to the curb, lowered the window of my van, and said Tim sent me to get *las langostas*.

The guy went bananas, shouting "no, no, no;" saying things *en español* that I didn't understand, and acting as if he didn't know why I was there. It was pretty clear that the deal was off. I apologized and drove away. I wasn't sure what just happened.

Tim explained later that the restaurant owner didn't know about the deal. His contact couldn't get the kickers for me because the owner was standing right there on the sidewalk. So, the hawker made a big scene and pretended that some *gringo loco* offended him by trying to buy *langostas* on the street rather than eating in the restaurant. All along, I had assumed that the hawker was going to pay the restaurant owner the wholesale price and mark up the lobsters about $1 apiece for us.

Now I wasn't so certain.

I Love Baja!

Chapter 8:
Baja Burgers

During my first months in Baja, I sampled Mexican cuisine at various restaurants. Imagine my surprise to discover a little roadside cafe with a big slogan proclaiming "The Best Burgers in Mexico." It was worth a closer look, so I pulled into the dirt parking lot in La Misión.

The place was named Baja Burgers, in a two-story cinder-block building painted bright yellow, with red flames painted from the ground to the top of the cafe windows. The slogan was in big red letters above the flames. You had to be blind to miss it. The glass door was open, and the smell of *hamburguesas y papas fritas* welcomed me.

The cafe dining area was about fifteen by twenty feet, separated from the kitchen by small counter and an open wall, so the cook could see the customers. A clear plastic jar sat on the counter next to the cash register, with a handwritten sign taped to it soliciting tips.

The concrete beam across the ceiling had the phrase "Free Burgers *Mañana*" painted in red. I like a place where the owners have a sense of humor. It had six little round folding tables, four with four folding chairs, and two with two chairs. I chose the two-chair table next to one of the front windows, with a great view of the highway. I could see and hear big rigs gearing down, pulling double trailers stacked with bags of cement for construction projects, straining to make it up and over the crest of the hill.

Everything on the handwritten whiteboard menu *en inglés* was either burgers or chicken, with one salad. No traditional Mexican food here. Rosa, *la mesera,* had a great smile and dimples, spoke a little *inglés*, and I spoke a little *español*. Together, we figured out that I wanted the #3 Baja Combo that included fries and a soft drink for forty-five pesos. Well done, of course.

Baja Burgers Interior, La Misión, Baja California

A couple of local *hombres* wearing cowboy boots came in and shouted their order to the cook without waiting for Rosa. Three other guys showed up, business types, one wearing trousers and dress shoes, the other two wearing jeans and work boots. A family with *el padre*, *la madre*, and *el niño* took another table. Hmm; very interesting. In just a few minutes, the place was half-full.

It was much better than fast food, and it was worth the short wait.

The cook, who was Rosa's sister, cut the fries by hand with the skin on and cooked them just right—not crunchy, not limp. The quarter-pound beef patty was well done, just like I hoped. It nestled on a fresh leaf of crisp lettuce to keep the bottom bun from getting soggy. A whole slice of sweet white onion sat on top of the patty, followed by a cool slice of ripe tomato with a dab of *mayonesa,* then a couple of pickle slices and just the right amount of mustard on the top bun. A long toothpick stuck through the top of the bun and fastened the paper wrapped around the whole thing. Obviously, somebody had put some thought into how to make a good burger. It reminded me of the quality control by In-n-Out burgers in California.

The concept for Baja Burgers came from Travis, an ex-Texan, and his friend Jesse (Jésus), a Baja local who lived with Rosa. They saw the niche for a great American burger in the land of tacos and burritos. The concept was to make fresh cut fries, use top quality beef and vegetables, and have Rosa put it on the tables for a reasonable price.

Jesse created what became the star of the menu, a top-of-the-line Baja Combo, with a whopping half-pound of ground round. It stuck over the sides of a fresh-baked bun from the *panaderia* down the hill in La Misión. He didn't use frozen beef patties, and Rosa's sister ran the round steak through a hand crank grinder before she put it onto the grill. For sixty pesos, including *papas fritas* and a soft drink, you couldn't beat it. It truly was the best burger I had tasted for a long time, probably the best burger in Baja, maybe the best burger in Mexico.

In 2005, Jesse and Travis dreamed of bigger things and opened a second location farther north in Primo Tapia about halfway between downtown Rosarito and La Misión. They opened a third one closer to center of Rosarito, where *turistas* at other restaurants were paying up to $8 for burger combos not nearly as good. Maybe they aimed a little high, offering upscale specialties that included California frills like avocados or mushrooms or Monterrey Jack *queso.* Those extras, plus more expensive rental space and hiring workers outside the family, boosted their prices above $7 in those locations.

Travis left for Mulegé in *Baja California Sur* after the U.S. economic downturn started affecting Baja in late 2007, and after fewer *turistas* came to Baja because of drug wars between rival gangs. Jesse scaled back to concentrate on La Misión, featuring a menu tailored to the tastes of locals. A faded newspaper clipping on the front of the soft drink cooler in La Misión attested to the dream of multiple locations.

The remaining cafe was where Route 1 turned away from the Pacific coastline and headed over the mountains to Ensenada through the hill country. The village of La Misión has about 500 houses sprinkled on the hillsides and the valley floor along a shallow river that runs into the ocean 500 yards farther west. The little cottage where I stayed during my January 2006 visit to Baja was on one hillside, but I didn't recall seeing the little cafe back then.

The narrow, old, two-lane road has no shoulders, and driving is a little like riding a roller coaster. Just before the entrance for a beachfront community called *Playa La Misión*, a sign saying *precaución* warns of the road ahead. Just past the sign, the road turns left abruptly and squeezes through the toll road underpass, where I once saw an overturned tractor-trailer truck whose driver failed to heed the warning sign.

Immediately after the underpass, the road makes a sharp right turn, curves up the steep hill, and twists into a tight left turn with no guardrail on the outside. My senses tingled as I realized I was about 100 feet above the river bottom and there was nothing but open space on the right side of the road. While going up the hill and through that turn one time in 2006, I met a truck coming down the hill. Its engine was braking to hold back one of those double-trailer rigs, with its left front wheel in my lane. I could still feel that chill.

Baja Burgers fed me at least once a week during my first few months in Baja. My *español* improved while talking with Rosa, the smiling *mesera*, and her *inglés* improved too. I learned a lot about Baja from Jesse, who stopped by the little cafe for dinner every night after working to help build the new liquefied natural gas (LNG) facility just offshore. He and Rosa lived in the apartment above the cafe with her son, about twelve, who often did his homework at one of the tables before they closed for the day.

It was a family business; sometimes the sister's daughter filled in as the cook. Rosa was in charge, greeting customers with that dimpled smile, taking orders, and putting food on the tables. She brightened everyone's day.

Eventually, I came to see them and their little cafe as real life symbols of people and businesses struggling to cope with economic twists and turns in Baja.

I Love Baja!

Chapter 9:

Distant Shores

After my first winter in Baja, I headed back to Maryland for a few months. People kept asking me what it's like on the Baja peninsula, on distant shores all the way across the North American continent. It depends where you are, I told them— like the parable of blind men trying to describe an elephant.

For starters, Mexicans are very friendly and foreigners are welcome. The country has some other distinct differences from the USA—affordable medical care for all residents (including foreigners), free college tuition for all students, no smoking in businesses or any public places, and a nationwide ban on any kind of guns and ammunition. There are many more differences.

Throughout Baja, there is a back-in-time feel, almost like the USA from 1940-1980. Sometimes, it requires a pioneer attitude to cope with the lack of infrastructure expatriates are used to back home. An unreliable water supply is one of the biggest problems in some communities and *luz* is a concern in some others. Internet service is iffy in many places. Public sewer systems don't have flushing power to handle toilet paper very well. Baja is constantly working on improving major highways and roads, yet many streets are unpaved and almost all secondary roads are dirt.

Telephone service is usually reliable, and wireless phones are everywhere. Mexicans use cell phones just as frequently as people in the USA, helping Mexican businessman Carlos Slim become one of the richest people in the world. The mail is unreliable and iffy, usually delivered by motorcycle, somewhat like a courier service. Three letters mailed to me from Maryland on different dates in December all arrived on the same day, six weeks later.

The yesteryear feel permeates financial transactions—locals use cash for everything. Checks are almost non-existent in daily commerce. The electric company, gas company, water company, and telephone company insist on cash. Every month, locals and expatriates scurry to make monthly payments at *bancos* or at utility *oficinas*. Immigration professionals offer to handle these chores for foreigners. Some Baja businesses offer credit for pricey items such as flat-screen televisions and *refrigeradores*—with stiff interest rates. Big stores, supermarkets, some hotels, and a few restaurants accept Visa, MasterCard, and debit cards. Cash is king for everything else including buying gasoline at Pemex, the national-owned energy company that is the only source of vehicle fuel.

The Pacific coast area of northern Baja is becoming more like the USA every year, particularly along the Tijuana-Ensenada toll road. This is where Donald Trump announced and abandoned plans to put his name on a luxury high-rise Baja condo project perched on a seaside cliff looking at the Coronado Islands, just south of *Playas de Tijuana*. Before the USA economic woes spilled over into Baja in 2008, thousands of USA residents jammed into this area looking for cheaper housing and commuting to jobs in the San Diego area.

That's one reason the San Ysidro border crossing between San Diego and Tijuana is the busiest in the world, more than 17 million cars per year, about 46,000 per day coming and going. Drivers can squeeze into any lane they want. Except for special access SENTRI lanes, it's jammed and no one gives an inch. A few drivers honk horns, shout at other drivers, shake a fist, or make rude gestures. Mostly, everybody just sits and waits.

Part of Border Entry Checkpoint Leading to San Diego, California.
UCC-BY-SA-3.0/UUpstateNYer *at Wikipedia*

Traffic inches forward for about an hour in twenty four lanes while dozens of vendors conduct a brisk business selling food and souvenirs. The smell of burritos and deep-fried *churros* mingles with exhaust fumes. Peddlers with pushcarts and plastic coolers walk between lanes of cars trying to make eye contact with the captive market. Almost every souvenir you can imagine is for sale. Some vendors offer blankets draped over their arms. Others stack ten or more straw sombreros on their heads. Still others carry miniature guitars or wooden religious carving in their hands. Beggars compete with vendors as traffic moves through the gauntlet. Some women strap babies in slings to their chests, stretching out their hands for a few pesos. Children show off their dancing or juggle three and four balls in the air.

Tijuana traffic police ride bicycles in the traffic sometimes to encourage the goodwill, weaving through the cars, SUVs, and pickups. U.S. Customs and Border Patrol officers check identification for each driver and passenger, ask a couple of questions, and search an average of one in ten vehicles chosen at random. There is another California crossing farther east at Otay Mesa primarily for trucks and a third one planned east of that.

There are some notable beaches on the Baja Gold Coast from Rosarito to Ensenada. However, much of the shoreline is rocky with rugged cliffs running down right to the ocean's edge. Some shallow waters are good for wading, but sewage from big pipes or streams sometimes pollutes the water. The surf is usually too cold for anyone except surfers in wetsuits. People have been surfing in Baja for decades, following the swells as the ocean currents push southward.

Pacific Ocean Beach at Km58 near La Misión

Before I retired, I thought Baja was all about tourism. I was wrong. The border region between Tijuana and Mexicali is home to hundreds of manufacturing plants - *maquiladores* - making cars, televisions, home appliances, and other items for the USA. A vast agriculture acreage growing produce for North America stretches southward from

Mexicali. A dairy farm is just north of Rosarito and a larger one is just over the ridge along Route 1 a few miles south of downtown Rosarito. You can't see it, but you can smell it when the wind shifts and blows from East to West.

Usually, the daytime temperature along the northwest Baja coast is in the sixties or seventies most of the year, like San Diego, with morning fog many days. Humidity is usually in a comfortable range all year. Winds from *el Océano Pacifico* cool the west side almost all the time and cause a small wind chill effect. Occasionally, however, the *Santa Ana* winds blow desert sand and heat toward the ocean, raise the temperature into the eighties, and cause a two or three day heat wave. The modest amount of rain arrives in the December-February rainy season, which locals call *las lluvias*.

Rosarito, with a population of about 100,000, is an expatriate epicenter with a robust cultural environment. It also has a party town reputation, a holdover from when college crowds used to arrive in droves during spring break and Christmas holidays. In the twenty miles south from downtown Rosarito to the village of La Misión, more condos are coming. For now, small individual houses and trailer parks survive along Route 1. The wide beach at La Misión features horse rides and people who let their dogs run off the leash to romp in the surf. This is where Route 1 begins winding across the mountains to Ensenada and its population of almost 400,000.

Some of the most spectacular ocean views in northern Baja are between La Misión and Ensenada on the Tijuana-Ensenada scenic highway. The four-lane restricted-access toll road hugs the hills, twists and turns, and has speed limits ranging from twenty five to seventy miles per hour. Until the toll road arrived, there was no road along this coastline. At Km88 on the toll road, a large aquaculture business at *Playa Salsipuedes* grows wild Bluefin tuna reserved exclusively for gourmet sushi. They catch the wild *atun* far out at sea in giant soft net pens and then drag the pens slowly at one knot per hour to the protected waters in the sweeping cove. Still in the pens, the wild-caught *atun* gorge on live sardines until they achieve the body fat content gourmet sushi eaters prefer. Reportedly, diners in upscale sushi restaurants on the West Coast and in Japan pay up to $18 an ounce for the Baja delicacy.[4]

Less than four miles south, *Playa Saldamando* sprawls along the bottom of the cliffs. It looks somewhat like Kirk Creek in the Big Sur area of California between Monterrey and San Simeon, with fewer and much smaller trees, and hillsides have more brown than green. A one-way dirt road winds down the steep hillside to a small beach at the ocean with black rocks worn round and smooth by the crashing surf.

Playa Saldamando (foreground) and Playa Salsipuedes

Campers can bring their own tents or rent tents and small camping trailers onsite at overnight prices ranging from $17 - $40 per night. A one-person-at-a-time hot shower costs

---

[4] San Diego Reader: 1703 India Street, San Diego, CA 92101; March 4, 2009

$3 for three minutes, and they cut off the water when the time is up. Old-style hanging kerosene lanterns rent for $3 a night, firewood is $5 per bundle, and a boogie board costs $2 for three hours. The reward for roughing it is a secluded area with about fifteen tents and a dozen camping trailers on the strip of sand, ocean surf in your face, and mountains at your back.

Surf on the western side of *Isla de Todos Santos* off Ensenada can be rough, tempting surfers to challenge waves sometimes as big as 30 feet. You can watch a six-minute overview from SurfMexico.net on the Internet.[5] *Bahia de Todos Santos* at Ensenada is big and calm and has lots of fishing boats, sailboats, and sightseeing boats. The harbor is deep enough for cruise ships whose passengers jam Avenue Lopez Mateo shopping for bargains in art, silver and leather, duty-free liquor, Cuban cigars, and European perfumes. Each year Ensenada hosts the Baja 1000 off-road race, along with the 125-nautical mile International Yacht Race starting at Newport Beach, California.

Surfing at Isla Todos Santos – Photo from ESPN.com

---

[5] http://www.youtube.com/watch?v=KgcfKRDtMZM

Tijuana and Ensenada also have European designer clothing stores, jewelers, upscale hotels, and five-star restaurants. Tijuana has very good French and Italian restaurants and claims credit for inventing "Caesar's Salad" in 1924. Ensenada is home to historic Hussong's Cantina opened by a German immigrant in 1892. According to local legend, a bartender at Hussong's invented a new drink in 1941 using tequila and named it the "Margarita" in honor of the daughter of the German ambassador to Mexico. Maybe.

A developing wine industry is emerging in the *Valle de Guadalupe* east of Ensenada. Wine expert Steve Dryden writes about the wines, food, and the valley on an official website.[6] More vineyards are south of Ensenada, along with thousands of additional acres of agriculture land growing crops such as strawberries for USA grocery shelves. Many vegetable crops including edible cacti destined for *tiendas de abarrotes* and *mercados* in Baja are in the valleys and on the hillsides. There are sizable farming and ranching operations along the peninsula. Most grass-fed cattle and poultry roam free without antibiotics or man-made diets designed to fatten them in pens. South of Ensenada, San Quintin proclaims that it is the tomato capital of Mexico.

Geographically, the Baja peninsula is long and narrow, twice as long as the Florida peninsula, a few miles longer than the state of California. It's almost 800 miles from north to south - half the distance from Maine to Miami - and 110 miles across at the widest part near the U.S. border.

Baja has a northern state and a southern state—*Baja California* and *Baja California Sur*. A mountain range, created by geological forces that also tore the peninsula from the mainland millions of years ago, runs like a spine down its center.[7] Winter snow blankets the tallest peak - just above 3,000 meters, or about 10,000 feet - in *Parque Nacional Sierra de San Pedro Martir* in the northern state.

---

[6] http://bajawineandcuisine.com/newsite/
[7] http://en.wikipedia.org/wiki/Baja_California_peninsula

Halfway down the peninsula near the state line where I took my first whale watching trip, a major international business produces barges of salt by evaporating seawater in hundreds of salt ponds. A website[8] describes it as the largest commercial salt evaporation project in the world, producing more than 7 million tons per year, sometimes at the rate of 2,000 tons of salt per hour.

After I moved to Baja, I learned more about the relatively unspoiled areas of the peninsula. The middle region includes 9,600 square miles of the *El Vizcaíno Biosphera Reserve*, which Mexico claims is the largest protected ecosystem in Latin America. It has coastal waters and mangroves, sand dunes, and arid high desert country.

A few hours south of the state line, *Laguna San Ignacio* is home to what may be the densest breeding colony of ospreys in the world. The protected area also includes a natural desert park (*Parque Natural del Diesierto Central de Baja California*), a 180-mile-long swath of high desert full of cacti and huge boulders.

El Requesón, the Sea of Cortez, Baja California Sur

---

[8] http://www.bajaquest.com/guerreronegro/baja15j_5.htm

The Sea of Cortez between Baja and the Mexican mainland has white sandy beaches and beautiful water in small coves surrounded by low mountains. It also has smaller cities and towns, many little islands, and a large variety of marine life. From Mulegé to Los Cabos, there isn't as much wind and it can be ten-twenty degrees warmer than the Pacific coastline in winter. Daytime summer temperatures often hit 115 degrees or more. That's when some expatriates head for the northwest coastline.

All the way around the peninsula, the Mexican government is supposed to protect the *zona federal* and ensure public access to the Baja shoreline. However, Baja represents some of the last remaining oceanfront land anywhere in North America and greed is a powerful force, especially in a country with an imperfect legal system.

The greed since 2000 is much like a tsunami, engulfing some of the most desirable coastal locations. Developers are taking over coastal *campos* on both sides of the peninsula. They are also usurping unspoiled oceanfront *Ejido* land the government set aside historically for indigenous farming communities, converting it into private land for developments. *Ejido* communities receive upfront financial benefits, but developers are the real beneficiaries.

Sand Dunes for Nesting Sea Turtles Near Todos Santos

Near picturesque Todos Santos, about thirty miles northwest of Cabo San Lucas, I visited three miles of oceanfront sand dunes previously set aside as a sanctuary for nesting sea turtles to lay and hatch eggs. Developers divided the dunes into lots twenty meters wide and sold all of them for prices starting at $300,000 US before environmentalists managed to block building permits.

Down south, on the outskirts of San Jose del Cabo, developers claimed a coastal area that included a lighthouse described in tour books and pinpointed on current maps of the area. It is still visible behind a new resort wall. A little farther north at Cabo Pulmo, developers are building a large community that threatens the ecosystem of the coral reef, one of only three living coastal reefs in North America.[9]

Back at *Playa Salsipuedes* north of Ensenada, developers installed a locked gate preventing access to the secluded area. The abandoned olive grove, steep dirt road, and rocky beach remain for now, but campers and kayakers have given way to plans for another upscale oceanfront community.

A little farther north, next to the government-built Puerto Salina Marina just south of La Misión, developers took over the beach behind the La Salina Cantina one night in September 2009. According to *el seguridado* for the cantina, they installed posts and strands of barbed wire between 2-4 a.m., claiming hundreds of meters of beach. They also put up a big sign declaring the beach private property and erected a plywood guard shack just beyond the fence. Locals protested and some expatriates said it was illegal. The developers did it anyway. Big money makes things happen in Baja, just as in the USA.

On the Baja Gold Coast, I can watch construction crews working year round to extend the path of progress southward. Bulldozers push aside businesses and homes to

---

[9] http://english.aljazeera.net/video/americas/2010/11/2010112765520766943.html

widen Route 1 into four lanes, starting just north of Puerto Nuevo and heading toward La Misión. Excavation machinery claws at the cliffs and dumps them into trucks to carry away. Giant road paving machines chew on cement mix, gravel, and water, then spit out new concrete four lanes wide.

I stop at the overlooks and beaches as often as possible, enjoying the spectacular views and sometimes scrambling over rocky cliffs to walk on the beaches.

Someday, developers will try to build multimillion-dollar homes clinging to the cliffs and nestling on the beaches of these distant shores.

Maybe they will develop the coastline on the whole Baja peninsula; maybe not. I know they will try.

Chapter 10:

July 4th Rooftop Fireworks

Like many other things in life, it seemed like a good idea at the time—an invitation for me to join Tim and four female friends and neighbors to watch July 4th fireworks from an oceanfront rooftop. Also, it would make a good reentry to Baja after being in Maryland for a few months.

Late in the afternoon, Sandy from down the street came knocking on the front door. Her friend Natalie had arrived early and given her a list to buy supplies and ingredients for the frozen mango Margaritas Natalie was contributing to the party. Mangoes, ice, and tequila of course; plus limes, some tortilla chips, and salsa. Tim and Sandy headed to Paco's Market a mile away. Sandy told me to take Tim's stuff to her place down the street. And to find the blender that Debbie left at Tim's place from the last party, whenever that was.

Tim's homemade baked beans were still cooking in the oven. A container of his homemade Coleslaw was in the fridge along with a two-litre bottle of Diet Coke®, ketchup, relish, pickles, two kinds of mustard, and a *gigante* package of hot dogs—enough for twenty people. Bags of other stuff he bought earlier with my $20 contribution were on the table —hot dog buns, plastic forks and spoons, paper plates, Styrofoam plates, plastic cups, and paper towels.

I loaded everything into the back of my van, steered around the potholes in the cobblestone street, and found a parking place near Sandy's oceanfront condo. SUVs and pickups with California license plates crowded the community—some belonging to renters, some to owners here for the holiday weekend. Up and down the street, music *en inglés y español* blared through open sliding glass doors on balconies. Mexico may not celebrate July 4th officially, but the holiday is an excuse to drive down from the USA and party in northern Baja.

It took me three or four round trips up and down the three flights of steps to Sandy's place, huffing and puffing and setting the stuff on the kitchen counter. Natalie was nowhere in sight. Sandy's two dogs were sniffing the food on the counter. I walked through the condo to the balcony with an armful of stuff, looking for stairs to the roof.

A metal spiral staircase was in a corner of the balcony. It was barely one-person wide, even for a slender person, an adjective that did not apply to Tim or me or his four female friends. Climbing it was like turning around a couple of times while trying to use a stair-climbing exercise machine. The pie-shaped steps were too small for my size twelve shoes and I had to walk on the balls of my feet on the way up and on my heels on the way down.

The basic problem with rooftop parties is you have to take everything to the top of the building. Which, I soon realized, was part of the reason the women invited Tim and me—to help get the supplies to the top while they laid out everything on the table.

It wasn't easy to climb up and down that spiral staircase. It was harder while carrying all the stuff from Tim's house, plus his Cole slaw and bowl of baked beans hot from the oven. It was still more difficult carrying Debbie's macaroni salad; Georgiann's potato salad, chocolate cake, and coconut cake; and two bottles of Sandy's red wine. My legs nearly wore out before everything was on the rooftop after several trips.

Debbie was sitting on a rooftop chair propping up her ankle she broke in January while walking her dogs on the oceanside cliffs. She lives in Baja all year and works from her condo as a telecommuter for medical billing back home in Denver. Her oversize designer sunglasses, tight-fitting top, and knee-length pants gave her the look of a femme fatale in her fifties. She had rescued a couple of dozen strays and found homes for them, and two of her remaining smaller dogs were nipping at each other and enjoying a romp on the rooftop expanse. Her third dog, Ali, was as big as a wolf and looked like one. He sat around looking up at the evening sky; I expected him to start howling after dark.

Sandy and her two dogs went up and down the stairs more easily than I did, probably because they were used to the climb. She owns a San Diego residential health care business for Autistic adults and manages it from her condo with frequent site visits across the border. She is sixty-ish, legally deaf, and has trouble hearing even with hi-tech hearing aids. In her youth, she rejected the idea that non-hearing is a disability and she travels the world on a whim. Four kittens she rescued recently had taken over one of her three bedrooms. She loves animals and is very funny. A bundle of energy, she's a slightly mellow version of Bette Midler.

Georgiann, in her early sixties, spends the summer in Baja to escape the desert heat in Palm Springs where she owns rental apartments. She zips around the community in a red Honda hatchback. Cheech and Chong, her twin dogs the size of miniature ponies, were a tight squeeze on the spiral staircase because they tried to climb up side-by-side. Zeus, bigger still, was reluctant to climb the stairs. She pushed him from behind and he made it to the top. Most of the time, she hires Tim to walk Cheech and Chong and Zeus or take them to the beach. Other times, she drives through the community with the dogs trotting along behind her. She isn't much of a walker.

Natalie sat at another table, waiting for Tim to put booze in the blender and render the ice, mangoes, and tequila into her Margaritas. She's about sixty, a real estate agent with inside knowledge of the slumping market along twenty miles of the Pacific coast. She was getting a little chilly in the rooftop ocean breeze with her bare shoulders, arms, and plunging neckline. She asked Tim to fetch her jacket from downstairs because she didn't want to make another trip up the stairs. Tim looked at me and rolled his eyes.

All of us were finally together, on a rooftop overlooking the Pacific, celebrating July 4th, and ready to watch fireworks up and down the coast. Tim, four of his female friends, eight of their dogs, and me.

The latest community news was from a few days ago when four vehicles full of Mexican Federal Police stormed a third floor condo unit on the other side of Sandy's place. They arrested the owner for having a handgun and ammunition, took him to jail, and confiscated his pickup truck. Private ownership of any firearms or ammunition is a serious felony in Mexico. The women discussed the irony of the recent U.S. Supreme Court decision about the Second Amendment. Debbie speculated the *federales* might confiscate the condo and she worried about the owner's wife.

Every so often Natalie asked Tim to make another pitcher of her mango Margaritas. He kept telling her they were papaya Margaritas because the market was out of mangoes. Pink Margaritas didn't suit my taste, although everybody else bragged about them. I sipped my Diet Coke®, munched chips and salsa, and listened to the stories. Tim kept saying he would start the hot dogs in a few minutes. Everybody started digging into the other stuff after a few more pink pitchers. It was good food. We ate almost all of it, except the two cakes, before the hot dogs were ready.

Georgiann's son John, about forty, arrived from Palm Springs with his own dog. He said it was 114 degrees when he left the desert. Now we had nine canines on the rooftop. All of them seemed to get along well enough.

"I didn't know it was a Bring-Your-Own-Dog party," joked Natalie. She mused that maybe she should go home and get her five dogs. I thought to myself that she didn't want to climb up the stairs again. I was right.

It's illegal to set off fireworks in Baja, partly because they might cause a wildfire. Of course that doesn't stop vendors from selling huge quantities to July 4th revelers who like to light the fuses and shoot skyrockets in an arc over the ocean. Just after sunset they began setting off fireworks in the Alisitos campground down at Km58, about a mile away. The view in the distance from our rooftop was nice.

Then somebody on the patio below us shot off a couple of skyrockets that exploded right in front of our rooftop, about fifty feet out in the ocean. The eye level view from the rooftop was spectacular.

That's when the dogs went crazy. They started barking and yelping, running around everywhere, looking for an escape route. Zeus tried hiding under the table at first.

Sandy's dogs got off the rooftop quickly, probably because they knew how to find the stairs. Georgiann took charge and tried to calm down the rest of the dogs and lead them down the stairs. She had trouble navigating the narrow spiral staircase and dogs began piling up behind her. John untangled the pileup from behind while holding onto his own dog.

Tim grabbed Cheech and Chong by their collars so they wouldn't trample anybody in the stampede. He released them after the stairs cleared. They stumbled down the stairs to join the others. Debbie was holding Zeus by the collar, saying she was afraid he might jump off the rooftop. Natalie kept saying she had to get home right away because her own dogs might be freaking out too and might destroy things in her house.

I was laughing and trying to visualize the bedlam downstairs with everybody sorting out all the dogs and getting them onto leashes before opening the door and leaving. In a few minutes Sandy came back up to the roof and decided to forget about cleaning up until morning. She and Tim and I managed to get the remaining food back down the stairs in one trip.

Tim said to put his leftover Cole slaw, baked beans, and the coconut cake into my van and head for home. I loaded everything and looked around for him. He was sitting in the back of Debbie's little Subaru Baja SUV, holding onto her dogs, as she drove away and headed for her place. He showed up a few minutes later at the house, flopped down on the sofa, and started watching Jaws 2. Both of us were exhausted.

"You know they invited us so we would do all the work," he said. "Women do that."

"Maybe," I said. "But some women just want to hang out with guys they like and know they can trust." He grunted.

Maybe he was right; I didn't care either way. It was a good party, a party to remember, although we missed the rest of the fireworks.

Chapter 11:

Perros y Gatos

One of the things I keep relearning in Baja is how much expatriates love their *perros y gatos*. Little dogs, big dogs. Sleek dogs, shaggy dogs, fluffy dogs. Kittens and cats of all colors and sizes. Sometimes it seems like almost every *gringo* on the Baja Gold Coast has a dog, or two or three, and many people have several cats. One friend has *ocho perros* in her expansive oceanfront home.

In Plaza del Mar, community streets become meeting places during morning and evening strolls as owners and dog walkers make their rounds, with as many as three or four dogs, usually on separate leashes. They exchange greetings and sometimes stop to chat for a moment. Beneath the surface, however, all is not well. What happens with that many dogs around is like a play in several parts - tragedy and comedy together - something Shakespeare might have written.

Cheech, one of Georgiann's twin 120-pound dogs, almost killed a fluffy little dog one morning in 2008. Tim was walking with both Cheech and Chong on their way to the beach when they rounded a corner and came face-to-face with Dan walking his little dog.

Unfortunately, all three dogs were off the leash, and Dan's dog was yapping as little dogs do. According to Tim, Cheech opened his big ol' mouth, clamped down on the little dog, lifted it off the ground, and shook it like a rag doll. Dan said Cheech was also banging it against the pavement as he shook it.

Tim got Cheech to spit out the little dog, and Dan carried it away in his arms. Debbie drove him to a Mexican vet to get emergency treatment for the dog. It survived, but it had neck wounds, internal injuries, and a broken leg. Dan took it to San Diego for surgery and to recuperate in a doggie hospital. I could give more details, but it would sound like I was making it up. Emergency care, surgery, and recuperation cost nearly $4,000, all of which Georgiann paid.

Chong, Cheech's good twin, became mysteriously ill later that summer. A local vet's first diagnosis of his illness included the possibility of rat poison. Immediately, Georgiann blamed the man who lived across the street from her backyard playground for her dogs. For a week or more, allegations flew back and forth about whether the neighbor poisoned Chong over a dispute with the homeowners' association, because Georgiann was president of the HOA. A sick and deranged deed, if true, but unlikely.

The dog spent four days at a vet in Ensenada, trying to recover. He returned home to recuperate, but he just lay around, became weaker, and had trouble breathing. A vet on vacation in one of the houses checked him and said to take him to the states for a thorough exam, so Georgiann's son John took him to an animal ER facility in San Diego.

Georgiann needed to move Chong from the ER facility to an animal hospital a couple of days later for follow-up care. Tim and I were going to San Diego for errands, so she asked us to transport Chong between facilities on the same trip, and she gave Tim $500 cash to cover the medical bill. Chong still had an IV catheter on his left foreleg, covered by a bright red elastic wrap. The place gave us some papers, x-rays, and a bag of IV fluids to take with him to the animal hospital. Tim asked if Chong had anything to eat that morning.

"No," they said, "Just plenty of fluids overnight."

Chong seemed happy to see Tim, perhaps remembering the morning walks on the beach before he became ill. He was a little wobbly and whined weakly, maybe with anxieties from being in and out of vet facilities for six or seven days. He managed to get into my Caravan okay, and he sat down on the floor in front of the second row of seats.

Enroute to the animal hospital, I told Tim about a roadtrip from Louisiana to Missouri a long time ago with one of Nancy's cats, when the cat jumped out of the car and we chased it for an hour or more. I figured nothing that bad could happen with Chong. I was wrong.

A few minutes later, we heard and smelled dog emissions. I glanced back and saw Chong squatting in the right rear captain's chair, looking at me.

"You wouldn't crap in my van, would you Chong?" I asked.

Tim said it was just a dog fart. But the odor was strong and got stronger by the minute. We opened the windows for fresh air. When we arrived at the animal hospital a few minutes later, Tim slid the van door open and Chong stumbled out, still on the leash.

"HOLY SHIT," said Tim, describing the scene. He repeated it a couple of times for emphasis, louder each time. I walked around to see. The mess was almost unbelievable.

It was everywhere—the seat back, seat cushion, the side of the seat cushion, the inside surface of the sliding door, the floor carpet, floor mats, and door sill. It was also dripping down onto the parking lot below the door sill. Imagine the Exxon Valdez oil spill, except yellowish-brown with a repulsive stench.

We took Chong to check in at the front desk. Tim told the woman at the desk that the dog had become sick in the van, and he needed something to clean up the mess. She gave him some paper towels and some sort of pellets to absorb liquids, and he went outside to clean up. I signed a bunch of admission papers, including a questionnaire asking me to describe the current condition of the newly arrived patient. I wrote that he survived the stay in the ER facility and had a lot of IV fluids overnight.

"Oh yeah," I told the woman, "He just finished crapping all over the inside of my van." She smiled.

Back outside, Tim was standing by the van in a sort of daze after realizing that the cleanup job was far beyond our capabilities. I joked that it was good that I hadn't wasted money washing and vacuuming the van a couple of days earlier.

He knew a place in downtown San Diego with a big car wash operation. I told the attendant I wanted them to wash the van and detail the inside, which he said would take three hours and cost $135. I said two hours, grabbed his clipboard, and signed the work ticket before he could change his mind.

He called over the supervisor and told him what I wanted. The supervisor looked inside the van and asked "*que paso?*" I said my dog was sick.

The supervisor touched the seat cushion and smelled his fingers, then shook his head. "*No señor,*" he said, indicating that his workers did not detail cars with dog shit on everything.

I said *por favor* several times and started negotiating, knowing that any delay would make cleaning more difficult. We agreed on $200, but the supervisor let me know that did not include *propinas* for the workers. I grabbed his clean hand and shook it with relief. He assigned five workers to the job, and they started removing everything except the seats for the driver and front passenger.

A couple of hours later, the van looked great and smelled like strong hospital disinfectant. I paid the $200, counted out $50 for tips, and shook the supervisor's hand again. We picked up Tim's building materials and supplies, went to the bank, and headed for the border. I was exhausted and needed a nap by the time I got home.

Tim and Georgiann were in the living room talking when I awoke about 4 p.m.. The vet at the follow-up animal hospital had called her because Chong was worse. He recommended sending the dog to a cardio-pulmonary specialist, because fluid was in the areas around his heart and lungs. The vet wanted her to come and pick up Chong and take him to the specialist right away, before he closed for the day.

Georgiann said she told the vet she had no way to move the dog before closing time, and Chong would have to stay overnight. She said she was in no mood to drive up to San Diego in the next hour and said her friends were wiped out from one trip to San Diego earlier that same day.

So the vet told her he would call a Pet Taxi service and have them pick up and deliver Chong to the new location before closing, all for about $20. I couldn't keep from laughing at the absurdity of the situation. Tim returned the rest of the cash to Georgiann, minus what I spent for the car wash.

Maybe all is well that ends well, as Shakespeare wrote, at least for Georgiann's neighbor across the street.

The cardio-pulmonary vet phoned Georgiann late the next day to say he had ruled out poison as the cause of Chong's illness. Maybe people will be embarrassed that they suspected the neighbor of such a cruel deed, and hopefully they would be more tolerant toward him.

However, it wasn't going to end well for Chong. The specialist removed a malignant tumor and didn't expect him to live more than a few weeks. Understandably, Georgiann was distraught, and her son went to get Chong and bring him home.

Tim went to see him the next morning, like visiting a friend who decided to die at home.

I could imagine how the play would end; everybody could. However, I hated to see the final curtain.

In the summer of 2009, Cheech attacked a little dog again. This time, Georgiann and Sandy and their six dogs were checking on the two dogs owned by Georgiann's son John, who wasn't home. That's right, eight dogs off the leash, one small corner house, with an L-shaped porch. I wasn't there to see what happened, but people said it was awful. They talked about it for days.

They said Cynthia, a tiny eighty-something sweetheart of the Arcos neighborhood, was coming toward the corner, walking her little dog. Suddenly, Cheech ran into the street from John's porch, made a beeline for Cynthia's little dog, and did what he did a year earlier to Dan's little dog. Chomp. Shake. Etc. The other dogs followed closely behind Cheech, like a pack watching a kill.

Cynthia started screaming and Georgiann and Sandy rushed outside. They managed to get Cheech to turn loose. Details of what happened next were sketchy, but Sandy said the little dog was hurt badly. Cynthia took it to a local vet for emergency surgery and it survived. Sandy said later the dog had deep puncture wounds to one of its lungs, broken bones, and other injuries. Georgiann paid the bill.

News of the attack spread quickly throughout the community, all four sections of Plaza del Mar. Because the dogs belonging to Sandy and Georgiann and John were off the leash, other dog owners began talking about making changes, beginning with enforcing leash rules. People started recalling other incidents involving Cheech. After two days of grumbling by the community, Georgiann decided Cheech's summer vacation was over. She drove him back to her winter home in Palm Springs.

"He'll just have to learn to live with the 108-degree heat," she said. Her two other dogs, with no known altercations, remained in Baja for the rest of the summer. However, she continued to "walk" them off the leash, driving around the community in her little red car and having them run after her.

I Love Baja!

Sweetie, one of Debbie's four dogs, disappeared one Sunday afternoon a couple of months later. She was missing when Debbie had to leave about 1 p.m. and didn't show up after Debbie returned at about 4 p.m. Debbie walked throughout the community for hours looking for her and drove around after dark using her headlights. There was no trace of Sweetie.

Monday morning, Debbie concluded that Sweetie wasn't going to come home on her own. More people joined the search, partly because people liked to help find lost pets and partly because all the neighbors supported Debbie's efforts in rescuing almost thirty abandoned dogs and finding homes for them. She asked me to make *Perro Perdido* fliers with a picture of Sweetie at the beach, telling people of the lost dog. Some people speculated that a "dognapper" grabbed Sweetie hoping the owner would offer a reward. So the flier stated clearly in big bold letters that there was a reward, **¡RECOMPENSA!** just under the picture of the cute little black and white Corgi mixed breed.

We used email to send the flier to dozens of people, asking them to send it to others. On Tuesday, I printed forty fliers in English and more in Spanish, until I ran out of ink. I posted them all over the La Misión area—two restaurants, two grocery stores, *la panaderia*, the veterinary office, *el granero*—and at entrances to gated communities. At the same time, Debbie posted them at similar places north. By Tuesday night, probably hundreds of people knew about the little *perro perdido*.

On Wednesday, Sorayda, the housekeeper for some of us, found Sweetie locked inside a rental condo one street away from Debbie's place. She was hungry and thirsty, but otherwise okay—she probably strayed into the condo while the renters were leaving. Debbie and I sent follow-up email messages letting everybody know Sweetie was home and thanking people for their efforts. Many people sent responses saying they were relieved the story had a happy ending.

Page 97

Debbie tried to get Sorayda to accept the reward money. She wouldn't take it. Many Mexicans are like that.

A couple of weeks later, Sandy learned that Piedra had killed one of the dozen feral cats who lived down the street near Pam's house. Luis, Sorayda's teenage son, was an eyewitness, almost. Apparently, it happened while he was walking Sandy's dogs and had let Piedra off the leash to run in the grassy area around the pool across from Pam's place. He caught up with Piedra, who was standing over the severely mangled *gata muerta.*

Sandy was in denial at first, not wanting to believe it, but there was little doubt. Blood was on Piedra, she told me, and scratches were on her nose and mouth, obviously from the cat trying to fight back. A couple of Mexican laborers in the neighborhood confirmed the story and identified her *perra blanca* as the killer of *la gata blanca.* She asked Luis what happened to the cat's carcass, and he said the workers just threw it over the edge of the cliff into the ocean. She was distraught about that too.

A couple of days later, Sandy said, Pam asked her about the incident. Pam was upset, telling her how much *la gata blanca* meant to her and other neighbors, who had named the cat Fluffy. Sandy took responsibility and said she scolded Piedra for doing something like that.

Sorayda, Luis, and the laborers were more understanding. They simply accepted all of it as conforming to the laws of nature in the animal kingdom. Sorayda even petted Piedra to comfort her.

"Bullshit, I told Sorayda," Sandy said to me. "She killed Fluffy."

It was clear Sandy was having conflicting emotions and was unsure what to do with Piedra. She gave Sorayda strict instructions to have Luis keep all three of her dogs on the leash when he walked them—Piedra, Cindy, and Coco. She also made certain the dogs did not go out of her third floor condo unit without her or Luis or Sorayda in charge of them.

Less than a week later, I saw her with all three dogs on their leashes for a morning walk and saw Pam drive up and stop next to her. They exchanged words and Sandy stopped by my place, very upset about the confrontation.

"She says Piedra killed another wild cat," she told me. "But I told her it wasn't true because Piedra hasn't been out by herself."

Pam accused Piedra of selectively choosing victims based on color, said Sandy, passing over cats that had orange fur, such as Sandy's cat Garfield. All the neighbors knew Garfield and the cat tagged along behind Sandy sometimes when she walked the dogs.

"Pam's crazy—dogs are color blind," fumed Sandy. Nevertheless, Pam seemed determined to do something about it and she told Sandy she planned to ask the HOA board to take action against Piedra.

A few days later, Sandy and Pam accepted a truce in their different perspectives with a nudge from other neighbors, some of whom noted the lack of evidence against Piedra in the second death. Pam acknowledged the problems inherent in harboring feral cats and Sandy expressed genuine sorrow that Piedra killed Fluffy.

She was still tormented by trying to reconcile what had happened and what to do with Piedra. She decided finally to have a trainer try to teach Piedra not to chase cats.

After Georgiann's term as HOA President ended, new board members decided enough was enough. They issued a new email guidance criticizing unnamed owners who had more than a "reasonable number" of dogs. They also warned residents that the HOA would try to catch unleashed dogs and take them to the pound, a fairly certain death sentence for animals in Mexico.

Georgiann, who never used leashes, was already back in Palm Springs for the winter and her dogs were safe from the new guidelines. As the only remaining residents with more than one dog each, Debbie and Sandy felt targeted.

I Love Baja!

Both of them genuinely care about any kind of animals, especially stray dogs and cats. They nurse them back to health, have them neutered, and try to find new homes for them in the USA. By herself, Debbie had rescued and found homes for more than thirty dogs and cats. But finding new owners isn't always easy or quick and they had seven dogs remaining between them - four for Debbie and three for Sandy.

Debbie's dogs stay out on her second-floor balcony much of the time; maybe that's how Sweetie was able to wander off and go missing for three days. Although they try to keep the dogs on the leashes during walks, sometimes an unleashed dog or two dashes out the door ahead of them. The bigger potential problem is that people they hire to walk their dogs are not as careful.

They have grown very attached to their remaining rescued dogs, and are reluctant to part with any of them. At the same time, they are distraught at the thought that someone would catch any of the dogs and take them to the pound.

Honey and Coco are the dogs they rescued most recently. Debbie's housekeeper and friend Lupita found Honey abandoned at a Tijuana water park, and Debbie nursed the skin-and-bones puppy back to health. Coco was pregnant and abandoned, living under a vacant trailer on a hillside across from Sandy's condo. Both of them cared for her and her eight puppies, found homes for them, and Coco moved in with Sandy.

It's a dog lover's dilemma. Realizing the gravity of the HOA email edict, they launched an increased outreach effort to find USA homes for both Honey and Coco. They drove them to their new homes, met the new families, and cried a lot on the way back to Baja.

Now they have only five dogs between them. Sandy has Piedra and her beloved Cindy, an old Spaniel almost blind. Debbie has Sweetie, Chiquita, and Ali (the wolf from the 2008 rooftop fireworks party). Ali used to belong to Ernesto, a former *seguridado*, but started living with Debbie after Ernesto died. Maybe Ernesto's daughter back in the states would take Ali after she finished nursing school next year, Debbie mused.

Both of them say they can't keep from feeling depressed about letting the rescued pets go, but they know it's for the best. Shakespeare was right—parting is such sweet sorrow.

There is a clear cultural difference in Baja between Mexicans and *gringos* in the way people relate to *las mascotas,* the informal Spanish phrase for pets. Gringos talk among themselves about the difference, but most avoid talking with Mexican friends about the sensitive subject to avoid offending anyone.

The most obvious evidence of the cultural divide is the almost total absence of leashes by Mexicans. In three years, I've seen only a couple of Mexican dog owners with a dog on a leash. It doesn't matter where—in town, in gated communities, at the beach, wherever. Lynnsie says she attended an event where Mexicans proudly displayed their dogs in little dress-up outfits, parading them on leashes. She agrees that is the rare exception. Debbie says she has seen a few Mexican dogs on leashes. She also agrees that Mexican dogs are generally unfettered. Of course, some *gringos* never leash their dogs either.

Mexicans visiting or living in Plaza del Mar let their dogs run loose and *gringo* residents scowl, but hardly anybody challenges the situation. A Mexican Rottweiler off the leash confronted me in the street on one of my afternoon walks. I looked around, saw the owner watching from his balcony, and reminded him of the leash rule. He called off the dog.

A second difference is that Mexican dogs are free to crap anywhere. With very few exceptions, their owners don't clean up after them. It doesn't seem to matter where. Dog poop is on the streets in towns and villages, on the sidewalks, in parking lots, in landscaped areas, in playgrounds, at the beach—everywhere dogs roam. Almost all *gringos* carry plastic bags when they walk their pets. Again, there are notable exceptions.

Maybe the word "roam" is the key to understanding the cultural differences, because the owner-animal relationship between Mexicans and pets does not appear very strong. Usually, most dogs roam anywhere they want—in town, along highways, on the beaches—without any indication of who might be the pet owner. In town, dogs sleep on the sidewalks, in parking lots, even in the streets. They doze in the shade of parked cars on hot sunny days, and bark at each other all night.

There are so many dogs living on the streets, I wondered at first if they have some special cultural status. I soon shed that notion after watching Mexicans treat *los perros* with indifference and animal cruelty sometimes. Part of the indifference includes not feeding dogs regularly and many dogs are malnourished as a result. Another part of indifference includes lack of medical attention for common problems, such as worms or other common illness, and only a few Mexican dogs have vaccinations. Many Mexican *cachorros* have distended tummies and many adult dogs have unhealthy gums. Part of the cruelty includes kicking or hitting dogs, or picking up *cachorros* by one leg.

A third major difference between *gringo* and Mexican pet owners is birth control. Mexicans rarely neuter *perros y gatos*. At first, I thought maybe it was a cost issue, but free clinics advertise their services all the time *en español y inglés*. Some Mexicans use the clinics, but not many. Maybe it had something to do with the traditional Mexican Catholic religious heritage, I thought. Maybe it's about trying to spare pets the pain of surgery. Some people say it's more about letting males keep their *cojones*.

"It's *machismo*," says Bobbie, Sandy's friend from San Diego, previously married to a Mexican *hombre*.

In Mexican culture, *machismo* also influences decisions on what to do with females in a litter. Rather than having females neutered, Mexicans simply get rid of them—just take them somewhere else and dump them. Maybe someone will take care of them; maybe not. Almost all the *perros y gatos* rescued by Sandy and Debbie in Baja were females. That's the same way people in the Ozarks got rid of unwanted female dogs and cats fifty years ago, especially if the females were pregnant.

Mexican attitudes in Baja toward cats intrigue me. For whatever reason, *los gatos* do not seem to enjoy the same status as *los perros* in Mexican culture. I noticed from the beginning of my visits that locals in Baja have very few cats. Mexicans tolerate *los gatos*, but nothing exists in Baja like the feline worship culture in the USA.

Sometimes it seems that predator dogs help control the cat population in Baja. All those unleashed Mexican *perros*, roaming free, chase *los gatos* for sport and kill them when they catch them. Piedra, part Jack Russell terrier bred for hunting, was probably acting on her hunting instincts. Hundreds of other dogs in communities and towns on the Baja Gold Coast may do the same thing frequently and effectively. Mary Jane, Idalia's pit bull, spotted one of Pam's feral cats on a walk one day and dashed toward it. The dog jerked Idalia off her feet and skinned her elbows and knees. Luckily, Idalia held onto the leash, or there would have been another *gato muerto*.

Also, I learned that the concept of litter boxes for *los gatos* is apparently foreign to most Mexican households. Most supermarkets offer cat litter, but it's not available in little *tiendas de abarrotes*. Bobbie learned this the first time she tried to buy kitty litter in La Misión for Sandy's housecats.

"*No es necesario*," they told her at the little grocery, and suggested that she use sand from *la playa*. In Plaza del Mar, that's exactly what Pam's feral cats do—they use the sand at the playground under the children's swings. Unleashed dogs simply crap wherever they are when the urge occurs, sometimes on grassy areas around the pool.

Another cultural difference I observed is the lack of sentiment toward dead cats. Back in Maryland, Nancy buried her beloved dead cats with tearful ceremonies. In Baja, pet owners like Sandy and Debbie also shed tears of anguish for deceased cats and buried them among the plants on community property. The Mexican laborers simply tossed Fluffy's carcass over the cliff.

Apparently, many Mexicans are aware of the cultural divide and talk about it sometimes. Mexicans can't seem to understand the way foreigners treat pets—letting pets live inside, snuggling up on sofas with pets, lavishing presents on them, cuddling and cooing to pets in baby talk, and referring to themselves in the third person as "Mama" or "Daddy."

Anna says a Mexican woman told her once that, because *Americanos* treat pets so well, she wants to come back in her next life as an American dog.

Chapter 12:
¡Feliz Cumpleaños!

Birthdays are special occasions anywhere in the world, whatever your age. It doesn't matter who you are, where you live, or whether you're rich or poor.

I went to a birthday party in August of 2008 for José Carlos, the five-year-old son of Rosella. As the only non-Mexican at the party, I learned a lot about family culture in Baja and made it through the entire afternoon *en español* without embarrassing myself (I think).

Her modest traditional Mexican neighborhood is in an area of town near the ocean in north Rosarito. The one main asphalt street has speed bumps and a lot of potholes, which have the same effect as speed bumps. Almost all the streets are dirt—it was the first time I ever encountered dirt speed bumps (*topes*). She lives on a street behind the main street, a couple of streets from the ocean. Developers haven't discovered the area yet, although a huge condo project is only a mile north. The house is in a relatively low-income neighborhood; however, nothing about the party or the people was poor. It could have been in a backyard in a suburban Maryland neighborhood.

The party was supposed to begin at 1 p.m., but I had learned that a starting time in Baja is approximate. Sure enough, I was the first guest although I arrived almost fifteen minutes late. I knocked on the open front door.

"I'm not ready yet," Rosella shouted from inside. "Can you play with José Carlos for a few minutes?"

He was sitting outside on the front steps, bored with waiting for the party to begin. I showed him how to stretch a balloon to make it easier to blow up, before he became bored with watching an old guy blow up balloons.

A couple of neighborhood boys older than José Carlos were hanging around, trying out his sister's skateboard, his Razor scooter, and his BMX bike with training wheels. One boy went down the steep concrete slope too fast, bounced into the dirt street, and bent the left training wheel brace. With the nonchalance of a possible future auto mechanic, he picked up a rock from the dirt street and beat it back into position. Then he pedaled the bike up the driveway and handed it back to the birthday boy.

The first person to arrive about 1:30 was Alicia, José Carlos' *abuela,* carrying two platters of homemade cupcakes from her back door across the dirt street. Icing in different colors, each topped with a construction paper car stuck onto a toothpick. She didn't like the layout of the six tables and thirty chairs. I helped her rearrange all of them so two tables for food would be in the shade of the wooden lattice gazebo.

After arranging the tables, Alicia took up position at a six-chair table in the middle of the patio and told me to sit there too. Three other eight-foot banquet tables surrounded her table on three sides, giving her a commanding view and place of honor at the event. Triny, from her office, arrived a few minutes later and joined us. The three of us nibbled on homemade salsa dip with tortilla chips while waiting for guests to arrive.

Each guest, children and all, came to Alicia's table first and greeted her with a cheek kiss as she sat. She introduced Triny and me to each of the new arrivals, and I stood and shook their hands. Most guests were families, bringing one or two children to the party, and carrying a big bag with one or more presents. Some children were classmates at José Carlos' preschool; others were children of family and friends. Most were from Rosarito; some were from Ensenada, almost fifty miles south. Rosella lived there until she left her husband two years ago, quit her job in a beauty shop, and moved back to Rosarito to start life as a single mother.

Rosella's best friend Alejandra arrived from Ensenada just before 2 p.m. with her daughter. Between then and 3 p.m. was when most other guests arrived. The street began filling up with late model pickups, SUVs, and sedans costing $20,000 and up. *Los niños* quickly went into the rented Moon Bounce on the second parking space and hurled themselves at each other with abandon, while *las niñas* seemed content to bounce up and down in one corner.

Shortly before 3 p.m., Alicia's husband Sergio arrived from across the street and joined us at her table. Rosella's sister Aurora and her husband Rafael and two children arrived from Ensenada a few minutes later, which seemed to signal it was time to eat. Alicia stood and went to the food table first, followed by the rest of her table and then the other guests.

The food was typical *Americano* backyard party stuff —deli-style sandwiches of ham and cheese, roast beef, and turkey on three different breads; potato salad, pasta salad, and vegetable salad; gallon jugs of fruit punch and lemonade, soft drinks, bottled water, and bags of purified ice. The hosts provided everything. One of the things that impressed me was the lack of alcohol consumption. There was one six-pack of Tecate beer, and maybe a couple of men had one.

After the food, people shouted *"Feliz Cumpleaños"* and sang the first two verses of *"Las Mañanitas,"* the traditional Mexican celebration song, which is the equivalent of singing Happy Birthday. José Carlos blew out the single candle in the shape of the number 5. He was into wheels, so almost all presents were toy cars or SUVs or motorbikes, or clothing with cars and SUV designs. Rosella made double scoop ice cream cones for all the kids and served the trays of cupcakes.

The last guests arrived well after 4 p.m., just in time for the *piñata*. No Spanish party is complete without a *piñata*. This one was a big homemade car that required several kids taking turns whacking it before it broke open and spilled its treasure of candies and gum. I left shortly after and don't know how long the party lasted.

My good friend Rafael back in Baton Rouge told me he used to go to parties like that when he was growing up in Colombia. He said a birthday luncheon isn't a success if all the guests leave before the sun goes down. Maybe it's the same in Baja.

About a year later, I went to a celebration for Charlie Wild's birthday, honoring the eighty-something iconic expatriate who has lived in Playa La Misión longer than most people can remember. The celebration was during the monthly "open-mic" amateur music event at the Half Way House cantina and restaurant, complete with Margaritas, beer, and appetizers.

Maybe fifty people from the local community showed up for the afternoon - a small sea of Americans, Mexican-Americans, and Mexicans - enjoying the festivities and capturing the occasion with digital cameras and cell phones. Another dozen people were there too, mostly in the adjacent dining room – some visitors from California and Arizona, some houseguests from as far away as Israel – observing all the excitement. Standing along the back wall of the cantina, I tried to explain it to a couple of them.

"This is Baja," I told them. "It's what people do here."

We had other birthday parties during 2009 for other local residents - Chef Johnny, Pat, Arthur, and Doug - all of them good times too. Many people at those parties were at

Charlie's party, but the other parties didn't have the same atmosphere as his event. I'm not saying his party was better —just different, partly because it was public. Saturday's talent show included two regular singer/guitar players, two conga drummers, a keyboard player, and Beth the local opera singer in fine form. An Arizona visitor got out his trumpet and did a good job on *"Tequila"* and *"Girl From Ipanema."* Chef Johnny led bi-linguals in singing *"Las Mañanitas."*

Happy Birthday Charlie!

Come toast Baja favorite

Charlie Wild

on his birthday during the open-mic program at Half Way House Saturday, September 12th From 4:00 p.m. to 6:00 p.m.

Not one but two delicious chocolate cakes by Molly Post and Janice Patten.

People have loved Charlie for years, since he and his late wife built a summer house on the beach at Playa La Misión in the 1960s for getaways from Los Angeles. They used to pack up their three sons and some supplies, and head for Baja in their station wagon with the plastic wood on the sides. Back then, he says, the roads south of the border had ruts, there was no electricity south of Tijuana, and the trip was more like an outdoors adventure. Over the years, more people discovered Playa La Misión and together they built a community. Charlie was one of the pillars.

I Love Baja!

Way back when, Charlie made his living as a commercial artist in New York City working with his father, who retouched photos. Charlie moved to Los Angeles, opened Wild Studio in 1959, and refined his techniques. He became a "craftsman savior" for Hollywood studios and ad campaigns, according to an Internet article.

Nowadays, he paints and draws at his beachfront home and teaches others how to paint. Bold seascapes and sunsets fill his house, along with portraits and sketches of the famous. Some of his art pieces sell for hundreds of dollars at charity auctions to raise money for educating underprivileged children in La Misión. Pictures of some of his artwork are in a little book he wrote about life in Baja, filled with folksy stories told with an old timer's perspective. He paid to print the book himself, and he carries a few books in a bag, selling them for $10 apiece to help raise money for the kids.

Arthur, a Hollywood screenwriter and one of Charlie's beachfront neighbors, jumped onto the stage during the birthday event to urge more people to buy the book. To interest people, he read a story from the book about a weathered wooden beam that drifted out of the ocean and stuck in the sand. For a time, it served as a friendly bench, picnic table, and beach bar.

The room turned quiet while people listened to the whole story, of how a violent storm tore the friendly beam from the sand. The storm turned it into an angry battering ram on beachfront homes, then swept the beam away. Everyone applauded, appreciating Charlie's writing style. He stood to acknowledge the applause, waving his hands.

Dozens of folks crowded around Charlie's table and shook his hand during the event, wishing him well. He stood several times for hugs and kisses from the ladies, danced with a couple of them briefly, and always sat back down next to his girlfriend Janice. He and she and their late spouses were a foursome for years. A widower and a widow now, they fell in love.

I Love Baja!

It was a two-cake event, orchestrated by a few of his closest friends. Molly brought a chocolate sheet cake with fudge icing, big enough to satisfy everybody. For good measure, a different Janice brought a round devil's food layer cake with just enough candles to make sure Charlie could blow out all of them in one breath, which he did.

When the event was over, Molly helped him gather his bag and the remaining books, tugging him and his girlfriend toward the door for another party the same evening.

"Charlie is leaving the building," Arthur shouted into the microphone. "Let's say goodbye."

The birthday boy paused at the door, turned to the cheering crowd, and waved both hands above his snowy hair. His blue eyes twinkled across the room; his smile touched all of us. We waved goodbye, locals and visitors alike, cheering and clapping, showing our appreciation once again.

As I said, this is Baja. It's what people do here. It doesn't matter if you're five, or eighty-something.

I Love Baja!

Chapter 13:
Baja Auténtico

Most vehicles in Baja have a look that is authentic Baja. The basic *Baja auténtico* look comes from several layers of dust, because even big towns and cities in Baja still have many dirt streets and secondary roads. People don't wash cars very often, other than the front and rear windows when buying gas.

A few layers of *polvo* are just a start. The next most important factor might be *llantas* that are mis-matched. My buddy Tim was the first to tell me about this, while I was shopping for a spare tire because my van did not have one when I bought it. He noted that all four of my tires matched and pointed to the car parked next to my van. Sure enough, it had two different brands of tires. He explained that most people in Baja bought only one tire at a time. *Llanteras* sell good used tires one at a time, usually for 250 pesos each. My spare and a rim cost 350 pesos including mounting and balancing.

Another standard component of any *Baja auténtico* vehicle is a religious artifact on the dash or dangling from the inside rear view mirror. I learned about this at the start of the whale-watching trip in early February. Later, I bought a shiny crucifix for fifty pesos and hung it on the mirror.

The most important characteristic of the *Baja auténtico* look is a few *abolladuras*. Actually, the more dents, the more *auténtico*. Most vehicles have dents, scratches, and scrapes. Many are also missing headlights or taillights, bumpers, mirrors, and so forth. As long as the vehicles still function, owners with little money don't fix dents or scrapes or replace missing items. Citialiti, the agent who sold my Mexican auto insurance, explained that only about thirty percent of Mexican drivers in Baja could afford to buy any auto insurance. Buying comprehensive coverage for self-inflicted dents is too expensive, so most Mexican drivers buy just the minimum liability insurance.

My van came with a couple of boo-boos, because Rosella had only liability insurance when she owned it. It suffered a good scrape and dent on the right rear corner earlier in the year after I backed into a wooden utility pole down the street in my neighborhood. *No hay problema*, as the locals say. The taillight, brake light, backup light, and directional signal still worked, but Rosella winced when she saw *la abolladura* and the black creosote scratches on her former van.

While I was in Nevada in the fall of 2008 volunteering in the Obama campaign, I backed into some very sturdy yellow iron posts at the end of my hosts' driveway and damaged the same spot more extensively. The entire red plastic light cover broke into five or six pieces, but I saved the pieces and kept going. *No hay problema*. I got some clear sticky tape and stuck the pieces together, then taped them back in place. Some Baja drivers use pieces of red plastic taped over the taillight light bulbs. Jacki, who has been in Baja for years, calls such fix-its "Mexi-rigging."

A couple of weeks later, still in Las Vegas, the left rear wheel of a big truck sideswiped the right front corner of the van while I was trying to change lanes. The truck kept on going, and I pulled onto a side street. The collision tore the bumper loose from the fender and bent my wheel so it angled to the left a little. The bumper was dragging the ground on the right side, and the entire right headlight was missing. I didn't want to risk leaving the scene of an accident, so I reported it to the police. By the time the motorcycle officer arrived, I already had the bumper back in place, thanks to a bungee cord in my emergency road kit.

On the Baja peninsula, you have to take care of things yourself because AAA and most other similar USA roadside assistance programs don't cover Baja. The Green Angels provide help on the toll road, but otherwise you need to be self reliant. Bungee cords and wire are like Baja bandages; locals use them to hold bumpers, hoods, trunk lids, or doors to vehicles. The police officer admired my handiwork and cautioned me to replace the light or I might get a ticket.

The cheapest estimate for the repair was from a Latino shop. Four workers conferred in Spanish, wrote down $2,000, and said four or five days. I thought, wow, I'm not in Mexico anymore. I called my insurance company, AIG-Mexico. They said to leave it at the repair shop and an adjuster would look at it in two or three days. I needed transportation, so I decided to ignore the police warning and started thinking like a Baja local. I simply got back on the road.

About a week later, my Las Vegas hosts Bob and Loya arranged for a backyard mechanic to repair the front wheel suspension and steering assembly. A front-end alignment shop discovered a cut in the right front tire. They said might it be risky and said the left front tire was wearing noticeably. They urged me to buy a matched set of four new tires, on sale right then for only $400, plus $100 for mounting and balancing. Fortunately, the Latino neighborhood had *llanteras* just like in Baja. I bought two good used *llantas* for $30 each, mounted and balanced. I laughed as I remembered what Tim had said about mis-matched tires, and realized the van now had three different brands of *llantas*. It was becoming more *Baja auténtico*.

Drive-by Latino mechanics in Las Vegas pulled alongside the van at stoplights sometimes and offered to repair the fender and bumper—the cheapest offer was $1,000. "*Muchas gracias*," I would say. "I live in Mexico— everything is okay."

The tires ran great, and I made it back to Baja without a ticket for the headlight. My friends at Plaza del Mar laughed at the sight of the van. It became even more *Baja auténtico* a couple of days later when I backed into that utility pole down the street. Yes, the very same pole.

"Did you get your driver's license from Sears and Roebuck?" asked Debbie and Sandy, who were with me. I was laughing too hard to say I learned to drive in Missouri, where utility poles did not attack vehicles.

Rosella was amazed at the damages to her former van and began working immediately to arrange for a trusted *mecánico* between Rosarito and Tijuana. I said all I really needed was to buy a new headlight and taillight, because the rest might cost too much. But she said to let her handle it. After she finished work on Friday, she said to follow her to let *el mecánico* look at the van. I tried to keep up as she zigged and zagged through back streets, but suddenly she made a U-turn in an intersection and I lost her. I doubled back and found her car in front of a neighborhood manicure shop; she was inside getting her nails done and giving directions to him on her cell phone. She's a great multi-tasker.

Roberto, *el mecánico,* arrived in a few minutes, and Rosella gave him a couple of air *besos* on the cheeks, holding her hands away to let the nail polish dry. She told me that she said to give me a good price—that I was old and retired and didn't have much money. He looked at the van for a few minutes, figuring in his head. Finally, he went to the shop door and they negotiated the price of a new headlight and taillight - not salvage parts - plus installation on Sunday after church.

It would cost about 1,300 pesos for the parts, plus 200 pesos for installation—less than $120 US total, at the current exchange rate. He planned to buy the new parts on Saturday, and I gave him 1,400 pesos just in case they were more than he thought. He guessed that the bumper and the fender might cost another 1,500 pesos. Rosella told him she would have to talk with him more before I committed to the rest of the repairs. She gave him a couple more air *besos*, with an *abrazo* this time, and he left happy. She has that effect on people.

About 12:30 p.m. *el domingo*, I met Rosella at her house on the northern edge of Rosarito to go together to have the van repaired. Roberto's shop was a one-room store specializing in audio components, not auto repairs, on a street close to the ocean in Playas de Tijuana. His father was waiting for us and motioned us into the single parking space in front of the shop. The new parts were ready, and Roberto installed both lights in less than an hour and replaced the bungee cord with four metal splints secured by screws.

Everything worked fine when he turned on the lights, and I dug into my pocket to pay him for installation, plus a 100-peso *propina* for fixing everything in just a couple of days. However, he declined *la propina* and he returned 200 pesos from the 1,400 pesos I gave him Friday. I was stunned.

He said the total cost was only 1,200 pesos, including installation, because the parts cost less than he estimated. That meant the total cost was only $91 US. I was having flashbacks to fifty years ago in the Ozarks where I grew up, when mechanics were family friends and did business that way.

I handed Rosella 100 pesos and asked her to give it to Roberto's father, but he declined it also.

I was beginning to think maybe I had offended them someway, but the father came up with a compromise solution. He told Rosella that his wife had just made fresh tamales in the apartment above the shop for *la comida* and we could buy *cinco* tamales for 100 pesos. Everybody seemed pleased and we embraced and shook hands.

"Let me know if the headlight points at the road or the sky," Roberto said to Rosella *en español*.

I Love Baja!

El Mecánico Roberto and Rosella with the Repaired Caravan

If I replace the fender and bumper, the van will still look *Baja auténtico*, just the way I like it. The fender and bumper repairs will not hide evidence of the accident completely. It will have the little boo-boos, scratches, and scrapes.

It will still have the black and yellow accent colors on the right rear fender and bumper. The crucifix will still dangle from the rear view mirror. It will still have three brands of *llantas*, and Baja *polvo* will cover it every few days.

In fact, only a few other *Baja auténtico* characteristics will be missing. One is a crack in the windshield. Another is a big $ symbol and a telephone number hand-painted on the rear window, indicating the vehicle is for sale.

I never tried to sell the Caravan, but I traded it for a 1996 Chevy Suburban in the spring of 2009. It's better for bumpy Baja backroads and doesn't bottom out on *topes* or *vados*. It makes a great portable storage facility and it's even big enough for overnight camping in a pinch. The sturdy SUV already had many *Baja auténtico* characteristics including four mis-matched tires, a couple of *abolladuras,* and a good layer of *polvo*. I liked it immediately. An online search confirmed the vehicle history was clean and it had never been in an accident. It was practically a steal, although it had a few defects.

The air conditioning didn't work, but on the northern Pacific coast of Baja most people just lower the windows. The radio was missing, but I couldn't hear music anyway with the windows down. The transmission had problems, and Rosella found a different *mecánico* to install a rebuilt one for only $700, one third of the cost estimate just over the border in Chula Vista.

On my first nighttime trip, coming home from taking six neighbors to dinner and a play in Rosarito, I discovered that the headlights did not function perfectly. The low beam lights were not very bright and the left high beam pointed too much toward *el cielo*. A bigger problem was that the headlights flickered on and off, so I turned on the blinking hazard warning lights to see the road better.

"You're freaking me out," screamed Debbie, riding in the front passenger seat, as we blinked our way towards oncoming traffic on the two-lane highway. A couple of days later, a roadside *electricista carro* charged only 100 pesos to repair a defective ground wire. I also installed fog lamps, just in case it happened again.

The sticker on the SUV California license plate indicated that it was time to renew the registration, which would cost more than $600. I asked Rosella if it would be cheaper to import the vehicle and register it in Mexico. She looked online and found that it would cost about $1,000 to import the vehicle and get Baja license plates—about thirty percent of the book value. Also, the Baja motor vehicle office would impound the vehicle for several days while verifying the ownership history. Therefore, I decided to register the vehicle in California to establish a clear title proving ownership and import the vehicle next year.

Not long afterward, a couple of Baja friends told me of another option. According to them, it's okay to operate a vehicle in Mexico temporarily with an expired registration sticker, as long as you carry documents proving that you own the vehicle. Maybe that explains why I keep seeing so many cars with expired registration stickers—one Florida sticker expired in 2007. It isn't entirely legal, of course, and Rosella cautioned me that *la policia* might demand a 500-peso fine, or maybe not. *El baile de la mordida*, you know.

An expired sticker on an older vehicle with either USA or Mexico license plates might be the ultimate characteristic of *Baja auténtico*.

Chapter 14:

Mexico Catches a Cold

The USA economic meltdown in October 2008 almost shut down the economy in northern Baja by late that year. "When the U.S. economy sneezes, Mexico catches a cold," as the locals say.

One of the most visible signs of economic illness in Baja was a glitzy condo project bearing the name of Donald Trump. Anybody driving along the toll road just south of *Playas de Tijuana* could see nothing was happening for almost a year. Even the billboard blew away, with Trump's picture and the slogan "Owning Here Is Just The Beginning."

Developers of the project couldn't borrow a dime to build the triple towers. The San Diego newspaper reported his troubles in Baja and *Forbes* magazine trumpeted it to the rest of the world. The last hope, some potential lender in Europe, turned down the financing. The real estate dominoes began falling in Baja, starting with that project and rippling south along the peninsula.

Apparently, the developer gave all the $32 million in down payments from buyers to the builder, who didn't build anything. However, somebody kept the deposits, and refused to return any of it to the buyers.

Trump's daughter, who said she was buying a junior penthouse suite, told *Forbes* that buyers shouldn't worry. The Donald would stand behind the project and he would see that people got what they bought. She promised that they would finish construction and deliver the first units in 2012— four years away. As you might expect, attorneys started lining up clients for class action lawsuits. As you might also expect, The Donald bailed out, distanced himself from the project, and sued the developer.[10]

Tiger Woods became the newest face of the truly rich in Baja in late 2008. Developers held a news conference at the Bel-Air Hotel in Beverly Hills, where Tiger announced that he would put his name on a 350-acre private golf resort named Punta Brava, south of Ensenada. Home sites would range from $3 million to $12 million. Partnership villas would start at $1.7 million, and individually owned villas would range from $3.5 million to $6.5 million. The resort would be on a secluded point of land stretching several miles into the ocean.

They planned to ensure safety for the rich folks by not having any roads for vehicle access. Instead, according to the *Baja News,* the resort would limit access to yachts in an onsite marina or high-speed yacht tenders to shuttle people back and forth from mega yachts in the Ensenada harbor. In a pinch, resort owners could land their private jets or helicopters at the resort's landing strip. As humorist Dave Barry would say, I am not making this up.

The economic situation was no laughing matter because it affected almost every part of life in northern Baja. At the same time, weekly news in the U.S. about shootouts and killings among rival drug cartel gangs almost wiped out the tourist business. The combination spelled d-i-s-a-s-t-e-r. Hotels discounted room rates by half or more, restaurants offered specials, and many shops closed early for the winter season. Others simply went out of business. Advertising was

---

[10] http://articles.latimes.com/2009/apr/10/business/fi-trump10

way down in free tabloids—the *Baja Times* slimmed down to half its previous thickness, the *Baja News* was down to eight pages. The *Gringo Gazette* was a distant memory. Times were hard for almost everybody.

Houses in Plaza del Mar were empty of residents and renters. Neighbors from Las Vegas, Los Angeles, Canada, and elsewhere stopped coming—partly because they worried about safety, partly because the summer season was over. Most maids and housekeepers in Plaza del Mar disappeared. Streets were almost empty of dogs. Georgiann was back in Palm Springs without Chong, who didn't survive. Sandy was leaving on a thirty two-day cruise with Georgiann and said I could stay at her place in return for taking care of her two cats; she would take her two dogs to stay at Georgiann's place in the desert.

In mid November, I headed for Baja Burgers. It was closed. The yellow building with the red flames was still there. However, the restaurant, Rosa, and Jesse were not around. I had a sinking feeling, fearing they had gone out of business. A couple of days later, I learned that they had moved down the hill and across the river and I went for dinner.

Their new location was much smaller. It was just a 10x10 foot kitchen behind a roll-up metal garage door, with only four tables and eight chairs in an open plywood shed out front. The shed had the same red flames and a sign boldly proclaiming that they still made "The Best Burgers in Mexico." I was happy to see both of them, and we shook hands and hugged.

I ordered the same top-of-the-line Baja Combo and it was as good as ever. However, little things were different. Unbranded red and yellow plastic squeeze bottles of catsup and mustard were on the tables now. Cans of *Coca Zero* were in the soda cooler rather than the bottles of *Coca Light*. Moreover, the newspaper clipping was gone from the front of the cooler.

Some big things were different, too. Jesse was

working at the cafe fulltime now; his job at the LNG facility was over after construction finished during September. Rosa was doing the cooking and didn't smile as much; her sister and niece were family victims of downsizing. Her son was still doing his homework at one of the tables. I didn't ask where they were living; the building didn't have a second story with an apartment.

I was the only customer between 6 and 7 p.m. We sat at the tables together in the chilly evening air, chatting about whether they should add hot dogs to the menu and buy a heater to keep customers warm now that winter was coming. The unspoken question was whether enough customers would come. They turned out the lights and closed early when I left. I was hoping they would make it through the winter.

A few days later, I went to visit La Fonda to sit by a little fireplace and have lunch. The bowl of black bean soup tasted better than ever, the tortilla chips flaked just as I remembered, and the homemade *pico de gallo* was still superb. Some things never changed. I added a fresh-ground cup of *café*, all for thirty eight pesos, less than $3 US for a great lunch.

I sat at a table next to owners Bonnie and Rich, chatting about what they were doing to cope with the fewer number of *turistas* during the off season. They were giving a twenty percent discount on the spa and discounting rooms to start as low as $50 a night.

Thursday night was now spaghetti night; a big plate with meat sauce, garlic bread, and salad, all for just $5. They also added pizza by the slice; draft beer was just $1. Margaritas and tacos were still just $1.50 each on Tuesdays and Wednesday nights, and you still piled your own toppings onto the *pollo* or *puerco asada* straight off the grill. Bonnie said the discount card they introduced for locals during the year had signed up more than 500 people, including me.

I told them about Baja Burgers. Bonnie said she hoped the little cafe survived, because she agreed that nobody could compete with their burgers. I was struck by the common business bond between the folks on the ocean cliffs and the folks down by the river. Both of them offered some of the best food around and both of them were looking for ways to survive hard times.

The Saturday after Thanksgiving, Debbie and I went back to Baja Burgers about 5 p.m. It wasn't open. We opted for Poco Cielo and enjoyed the special of clams fresh from the ocean with some kind of great sauce. Cheryl, the owner, was planning to expand with an open-air *palapa* area next door. We recognized a woman who used to work at the restaurant in the Hotel La Misión; she was waiting for her husband, who was a waiter Poco Cielo. She said Hotel La Misión planned to reopen in April after remodeling, and they were thinking of getting rid of the little trailers and building some condos. Even in hard times, apparently people clung to their hopes and dreams.

I tried Baja Burgers again the next week for supper *el miércoles*. It wasn't open that day either. On the third try, for lunch, I noticed that somebody had started removing plywood from the backside of the little shed out front.

The little restaurant with the big slogan was out of business. Maybe it would be back in the spring, maybe not.

I Love Baja!

Chapter 15:

Mexican Justice

One of the things I learned about the Mexican legal system is that it doesn't always provide a satisfactory result for everyone who seeks justice. Just ask people about Mexican real estate developments that don't finish construction.

There is even a phrase *en español* to describe the situation—*no siempre puedes tener lo que quieres*—you can't always get what you want. I know that's a song title from the album "40 Licks" by the Rolling Stones. But it's also in my nice *inglés-español* dictionary, right there on page 292.

If something goes wrong back in the USA, you can contact a consumer protection agency, seek mediation and binding arbitration, get a lawyer, or seek other relief. For serious matters, you can call the police. The U.S. system works most of the time and usually it produces a result in a predictable time period. Again, it may not be what you want, but at least it's a result.

By contrast, two traditions from the old world influence the Mexican justice system—*"jurisprudencia"*[11] dating to the 16th century, and *mañana*.

---

[11] http://www.law.arizona.edu/Library/Research/Guides/mexicanlegalsyst em.cfm?page=research

The essence of Mexican civil law is similar to Napoleonic Code in that it doesn't follow precedents, which I learned about as a journalist in Louisiana in the late 1960s. In many countries, the legal system accumulates court decisions and uses them as the basis for deciding new cases. In Mexico, using "*jurisprudencia*," the courts decide each new case without relying other cases. It doesn't matter whether you're Mexican or a foreigner.

For most cases, Mexico doesn't have a real discovery process, oral testimony in open court, or jury trials. In civil cases, the plaintiff submits a written statement *en español* and the defendant responds in a written statement. Rulings come from the judge who conducts a final hearing, usually seated at a small table in a small room. Both parties sit across the table, in case *el juez* wants to clarify something face-to-face.

After a year or so in Baja, I began to understand that *mañana* does not mean "tomorrow" literally, despite what my *inglés-español* dictionary says. The real meaning is more like "later," or "some other time." This is especially true in the civil justice system. Mexico simply doesn't have enough courts or judges to hear complaints and issue rulings in a reasonable time frame. One attorney says sometimes people wait five years or more for a decision.

In 2008, Mexico began an eight-year transition to a legal system more like the USA, particularly for criminal cases.[12] Until then, the combination of these factors is a triple whammy—not relying on precedents, no discovery process, and *mañana* that never seems to come.

I learned a little more about the Mexican legal system one day thanks to Tim, who had moved to Cantamar near Primo Tapia. On his early morning walk one Sunday, he saw a kid breaking into a neighbor's *casa*. According to Tim, the youth had crawled halfway through a small window on the side of the house. He just walked over, grabbed the boy by his belt,

---

[12] http://www.nytimes.com/2009/04/25/us/25prosecute.html

pulled him out of *la ventana*, and pinned him on the ground. The would-be thief protested, saying he was working on *la casa*. However, Tim said nobody in Mexico works at 6 a.m., especially *el domingo*, and usually they don't enter through the window.

He made the kid clasp his hands behind his neck, walked him to Tim's house, and used duct tape to bind the boy's hands behind his back. Then he marched him up the street to *el seguridado* at the front gate. The guard called for help, and *la policia* from the nearby police station in Primo Tapia took the kid into custody.

Everybody in Cantamar who heard about it hailed Tim as a hero, as did I. However, Tim said a couple of days later, he learned from *el seguridado* that *la policia* had to release the boy.

First of all, the kid didn't actually steal anything, because Tim caught him going into *la casa*.

Second, in Mexico, property owners are the only persons who can file a complaint with *la policia*. The absentee owners of the house lived somewhere in the USA.

Third, if somebody located the owners, they would have to appear in person at *la comisaria* to file the complaint. Of course, the owners didn't witness what happened, so how could they file a complaint?

No siempre puedes tener lo que quieres.

I Love Baja!

Chapter 16:
On the Road

After returning to Baja in early January 2009, I began serious planning for an extensive roadtrip to *Baja California Sur*. Sandy and Debbie wanted to tour the southern state and look for a warmer place to spend next winter and I planned to go with them.

We plotted a nineteen-day trip down Route 1, Baja's Transpeninsular Highway, to the southern tip in the Los Cabos area, around the cape, and north back home. The highway crisscrosses the peninsula several times, linking major towns on *el Océano Pacífico* and *el Mar de Cortez*.

We left La Misión January 31, hoping to take as many dirt roads as possible to explore the coastline and mountains. We stayed overnight in Lazaro Cardeñas, still in the northern Baja state, three or four miles down a sandy road at a protected cove on the Pacific. A few sailboats were docked for the night, with one family on a three-month journey. I bought a hand-woven blanket from a vendor on the dock for 150 pesos ($10.71 US at the time), because the nighttime low would be about fifty degrees and my room had no extra blankets.

Back on Route 1 south through miles of strawberry fields and vineyards, we crossed the state line into *Baja California Sur,* stopped at Guerrero Negro for lunch, and switched to Mountain Time zone. We arrived at San Ignacio about 4 p.m. to the sight of thousands of date palm trees, a little town square, and the sweet smell of oranges from orange trees beside the imposing cathedral on one side of the square. One of the tour books[13] says the church is one of the best-preserved missions in Baja, built in 1786 with money from the Queen of Spain.

The climate was warmer, and we decided to arrange a whale tour at *Laguna San Ignacio* for the next day from Antonio Eco Tours on the square, whose assistant led us on motorbike to an inn on a back street. It took ninety minutes the next morning to drive forty miles on bumpy dirt road from town to *Laguna San Ignacio*, where Antonio fitted us with life jackets and loaded us into a *panga.*

We saw many *ballenas gris*, some as close as ten feet, but not close enough to touch. I lost count after fifty. Lots of dolphins came close to us; some swam next to boat and under it. Some playful whales jumped straight up in the water, about one-quarter of their bodies out of the water. Antonio's wife and son cooked a late *comida* of fresh scallops, which we ate in a wooden yurt structure on the lagoon's edge. Afterward, we headed across peninsula to *el Mar de Cortez.*

We planned to stay overnight in Santa Rosalia, founded by the French in the 1880s, but were disappointed with motels and left after touring the town for about an hour. One notable feature of the town is that it has mostly wooden buildings, unlike most of Baja that uses concrete or concrete blocks and stucco. I wondered where they got the timber for construction.

The town also has a notable little church, the *Iglesia de Santa Barbara*, designed by Gustave Eiffel, who designed

---

[13] Eyewitness Travel: Mexico, Dorling Kindersley Publishing, Inc.; 375 Hudson Street, New York, NY 10014; 2006; p. 165

the Eiffel Tower in Paris. According to the tour book,[14] the church was a prefabricated metal church, shipped to the town in 1895. If they could ship a church all the way from Europe, shipping timber from someplace must have been relatively easy.

We made it to Mulegé for the night. The next morning, we went looking for a little restaurant called La Casa de Pancho Villa, where *Rio Mulegé* runs into the Sea of Cortez. Rob, the spa manager at La Fonda, told Debbie that's where Travis went after leaving Baja Burgers. It was tiny and rudimentary, just four tables, a *palapa* thatched roof, and *el bano* behind it. To flush the toilet, you had to dip water from a barrel with a bucket. However, it had two redeeming features. One was fresh squeezed *jugo de naranja*. The other was Pancho's daughter Emilia, one of the prettiest *señoritas* in Baja - maybe all of Mexico - with incredibly beautiful brown *ojos*.

El Coyote on the Sea of Cortez, South of Mulegé

South of Mulegé, we stopped at several picturesque coves with sandy beaches along *Bahía de Concepćion*. It was about seventy-five degrees by early afternoon, and we walked

---

[14] Ibid; p. 168

on the beach, visiting with campers in RVs from Great Lakes states and several places in Canada, who paid only $7 per day to live right on the beach.

By late afternoon, we made it to Loreto, which claims to have great sportfishing. Our hotel rooms were above a hardware store, with a balcony overlooking the street as in the French Quarter of New Orleans. A block away was the restored *Misión Nuestra Señora de Loreto*, a historic mission from the late 1600s that was the first mission in the Californias. That was back when Mexico stretched from the southern tip of the Baja peninsula all the way to the northern border of what is now the state of California in the USA.

A lot of fishermen and tourists were in town, drawn to Augie's Bar and Bait Shop. It's a waterfront hangout on the *Malécon* for *Americanos* and Canadians swapping fish tales enhanced by Tequila and beer and wine. It has a noisy bar on the street level, with a quieter little open-air restaurant upstairs.

Augie is larger than life. He sat at our table in the bar for a few minutes to schmooze and took an immediate interest in Sandy. We pulled a couple of tables together to visit with others and stayed longer than we planned. The hot pink T-shirt with Augie's logo looked really good stretched over the torso of the barmaid, and Sandy wanted to get one for herself. Augie said he would find one. All of us became good friends by closing time and Augie offered to buy breakfast and show us around town.

The next morning, Sandy didn't feel like having breakfast or going sightseeing. I went to tell Augie we would skip the day and be back that evening, and he was a little disappointed. He brightened up when I said we wanted to celebrate Debbie's birthday by having dinner there.

"We do it Mexican style," he said, with a grin. I looked at him quizzically. He explained that meant he would push Debbie's face into the cake after she blew out the candles. I didn't know Debbie that well, and I wasn't certain she would appreciate it as much as the crowd.

"Better let me check with her on that and get back to you," I said. He agreed to make the cake and wait for my feedback about the little ceremony.

Back at the hotel, I found a note on my room door saying Debbie and Sandy were taking the day off and going to find a spa. I visited museums, bookstores, an Internet cafe, some shops with ceramics and local art, and checked out a couple of places to rent next winter. The daytime temperature was in the low-mid eighties, almost twenty degrees warmer than back in La Misión, and it felt good. Apparently many others from north of the border liked it also. About one-third of vehicles parked on the streets had license plates from California, Arizona, Colorado, Utah, Idaho, Washington, Oregon, British Columbia, and Alberta; the rest were from Mexico.

Sandy and Debbie knocked on my door when they were ready to go to Augie's. Rejuvenated by the spa, they had the look of "Cougars" on the prowl, something you can read about on the AARP website. They looked *muy caliente* and turned heads when we entered the cafe. Augie sidled up to Sandy right away and got us a table in a prominent place, but he was noticeably cool.

"We're just friends, right?" he said to her, with his mouth close to her hearing aid. She gave him a funny look, but agreed with a smile. We noticed that he was schmoozing with a couple at the bar a few feet from our table. Curiosity got the best of Sandy after a bit and she pushed her way between them to visit. Turned out, they were good friends with Augie back in Oregon or Washington and just arrived. After a couple of drinks with Sandy, they said it was too bad Augie's girlfriend back there couldn't make the trip with them, because she really would like Sandy. Soon after that, Sandy decided she wanted to go somewhere else for dinner.

I knew Debbie was looking forward to the birthday cake, having agreed to just a little cake in her face. I hustled upstairs and found Augie. I said we needed to do the cake NOW, and he brought it downstairs. He handled the Mexican style just right and added a clever touch by proclaiming to the crowd that the occasion was the anniversary of Debbie's twenty-ninth birthday.

Before leaving Loreto the next day, we decided to hire a guide for a small boat to go sightseeing and snorkeling at nearby *Isla del Carmen* and *Isla Coronado*. I wasn't feeling well and I really regretted missing the boat trip, especially when the guide said afterward it was the most exciting trip he had in eighteen years. Sandy said that about fifteen minutes after Debbie got back into the boat after snorkeling amid sea lions and dolphins, a dozen or so Orca killer whales chasing dolphins came so close to the boat the guide was afraid the small boat would capsize. Debbie in her wet suit looked like a sea lion, said Sandy, and Orcas eat sea lions and dolphins for lunch. In fact, the Orcas caught one and ate it right then.

"She freaked out," says Sandy.

Malécon at La Paz

We stopped overnight at La Paz back on the Sea of Cortez, the capital city of *Baja California Sur*, where afternoon temperatures were in the high seventies. The hotel in the guidebook was closed for renovations although it was the high season, and we stayed in a so-so place over a very good Chinese restaurant. Before and after dinner, we strolled along the very nice three-mile *Malécon*. There were interesting museums the next morning, lots of businesses, busy local traffic, but not many tourists. Away from the waterfront, the city was too big for us and we moved on after one night.

We arrived during the afternoon at Todos Santos, back on the Pacific Ocean, close to the Tropic of Cancer. It was beautiful, about seventy five degrees, with Pacific Ocean breezes, many galleries, small shops, and several fine restaurants. According to a magazine article,[15] the area was once a prominent sugar cane farming center nestled against the western slopes of the *Sierra de la Laguna* Mountains and has a large green belt, organic crops, and freshwater springs. In October 2006, Todos Santos became one of only a few small towns in Mexico that received the prestigious designation of "*Pueblo Magico*"—a magical town. This is based on increased awareness of town planning, respect for historical architectural style, and strict design codes for any new buildings in the downtown area.

The annual February *festival de arte* was in town while we were there and most hotels were full, with no room at the Hotel California. The desk clerk, originally from Canada, said maybe the hotel inspired the hit song by the Eagles, maybe not. She said hundreds of thousands of tourists stopped to take pictures each year. (Don Henley, who wrote the lyrics, says the hotel had nothing to do with the song.[16]) We found good rooms above a laundry across the street in a funky little hotel where surfers were staying.

After staying in Todos Santos another night, we explored the beaches farther south at *Playa Cerritos*, which hosts an annual surfing competition with surfers from as far away as Hawaii and Australia. The Tropic of Cancer crosses

[15] Baja Traveler, Annual IX, 2007-2008 collectors' edition, Traveler Publications, P.O. Box 210485, Chula Vista, CA 91921.
[16] Baja Legends; Niemann, Greg; Sunbelt Publications; San Diego, CA; 2002; p. 243

the peninsula just south of Todos Santos, and the Japanese current makes the water warmer below that line—maybe eighty degrees. Many surfers don't wear wetsuits, a big change from sixty-degree water in northern Baja.

On the way to the Los Cabos area the next day, we drove into the mountains south of Todos Santos looking for a tiny place called Candelaria, where Debbie's tour book said a half dozen potters worked from their homes. There were many dusty crossroads without signs, and several cattle, horses, and goats. They either blocked the roads or caused Debbie and Sandy to shriek and tell me to stop so they could take pictures.

We lost our way several times before we found a rancher to lead us to the tiny village after forty eight miles on bumpy mountain roads, and we rewarded him with cold beer from the cooler. We found two potters—an enjoyable and worthwhile venture. Debbie and Sandy bought primitive clay pots from one potter named Carmen, who fired the pots in a kiln using dried cacti as firewood. Her daughter used a nail to scratch Carmen's name on the bottom of the pottery they bought.

Sign on Fence at Carmen's House, a Potter at Candelaria

We headed out of the mountains toward the ocean and drove past touristy Cabo San Lucas to San Jose del Cabo for the night. In San Jose del Cabo, *la policia* stopped us and told us Sandy's vehicle license registration was expired, the second time this happened on the trip. Sandy started fuming and insisting that they were wrong. Debbie had to make nice with them, especially after they took her to the rear of the SUV and pointed to the expired December 2008 registration sticker on the rear license plate. Eventually they let us go with a verbal warning. Maybe they checked to see if Sandy's vehicle was stolen, or maybe it was Sandy's scowl and Debbie's charm.

The next morning we drove toward the East Cape area on the Sea of Cortez looking for the dirt road along the coast, however we couldn't find the road to the lighthouse at *La Placitas*. We asked the European owner of *Casas Delfin* for help and she said developers stole the old beach road. She repeated it to make sure we understood what a bad thing they did—"They stole the road." She led us back toward San Jose del Cabo and directed us to the paved road north until we came to an unmarked dirt road leading to the beaches.

East Cape Coastline on the Sea of Cortez

Soon we were among unspoiled beaches and beautiful views, with very few houses, on the part of the old dirt road they had not yet stolen along the coast. We realized what she meant was that developers of beachfront resort hotels back toward town had simply included the old road inside their walled and gated resort compounds, and then built a new paved road outside their properties.

At Vinorama, we stopped at a seaside cafe named the Crossroads Country Club, a small open-air cafe with tables and chairs on the sand overlooking the Sea of Cortez. We watched humpback whales jump out of the water and crash backwards into the sea 100 meters offshore. Farther up the coast, we strolled on the beach at *Parque Nacional Cabo Pulmo*, which has one of only three living coral reefs in North America. Steinbeck described it in his "Log From the Sea of Cortez,"[17] and it had become a diving destination on *el Mar de Cortez*. We drove on to Los Barilles for the night, planning to keep going on to La Paz the next day, but we looked at the guidebooks and maps and decided to backtrack.

Cove at Parque Nacional Cabo Pulmo on the Sea of Cortez

---

[17] Log From the Sea of Cortez; Steinbeck, J.; Viking Press; 1941

Back at Cabo Pulmo, we rented a two-bedroom beach casa from Pepe's Dive Center, which operates from a *palapa* hut on the side of the main dirt road. Debbie went snorkeling at *Las Fraille* from 11 a.m. to 6 p.m., and I went sightseeing along beaches and coves. A guide named Mémo latched onto Sandy and took her and me to see several places to rent for next winter. He also pointed out real estate for sale, ranging from $20,000 US for quarter-acre vacant lots up on the hills to $12 million for an oceanfront mansion. A $200,000 place with beautiful landscaping was enticing, but would require truckloads of water. Morning at the casa revealed no hot water and not enough solar electricity to make coffee.

After the stay in Cabo Pulmo, we drove back to La Ribera and stopped to take pictures of a beautiful cemetery in the main part of town. It was big, well maintained, and all the graves decorated with elaborate and colorful paper floral arrangements. Many gravesites were in concrete block structures above ground, with roofs and doors, painted in bright Mexican colors. Iron fences and gates enclosed others —a celebration of color compared with drab above ground gravesites in the USA.

Cemetery at La Ribera

Back on Route 1, we cut across to La Ventana on *la Mar de Cortez* just south of La Paz. The windy bay had incredibly beautiful water that changed colors depending on time of day. Kayakers, windsurfers, and kite boarders filled the small village, most of them from Canada. Casa Verde had the only rooms available, with upscale teepees for $50 a night and a suite for $170. Luckily, the place was not full, so Sandy and Debbie negotiated $110 for a large suite and we split the cost. It was the Taj Mahal compared with most other places we stayed. The owners David and Alia moved there from Washington and started building individual *casitas*, each named for one of their six daughters. The suite where we stayed was named after Alia.

Kiteboarders and Windsufers at La Ventana

We backtracked down Sea of Cortez the next day to visit an historic bay named *Bahía de los Muertos*[18] on the maps and in the tour books. We couldn't find it. We learned that developers had renamed it *Bahía de los Sueños*[19] after buying all the surrounding mountains and beach to develop a

---

[18] Bay of the Dead
[19] Bay of Dreams

resort with airstrip, marina, and golf course. I understood perfectly—if developers could steal part of the old beach road down south, there wasn't anything to stop them from renaming an entire bay farther north.

The beach club restaurant was nice. However, the resort project had stalled with nothing but sticks in the sand marking unsold lots. The slick brochure was brutally candid: "*Plans to build out this project as proposed are subject to change without notice or obligation.*" In Mexico, that means they will keep all your money even if they don't build anything.

The next morning, we drove west across the peninsula on the way to Puerto San Carlos. It turned out to be a small fishing village with barrier islands just offshore, primarily dependent on income from visitors taking whale tours at *Bahía de Magdelena*. The *Gringo Gazette* newspaper in Cabo San Lucas had a story saying forty whales had arrived. Apparently, many tourists in the Los Cabos area read the story and decided to rent cars and drive six hours to see the whales because the half dozen motels in the tour book were full the day we arrived.

The only rooms available were at a little place run by three people in their eighties who lived in two units. Rooms were only 150 pesos for single occupancy, the same price as my new blanket the first night on the road. Other overnight visitors began to fill up the thirteen tiny rooms surrounding the enclosed courtyard, and the old folks seemed overjoyed with their good fortune. The black-and-white TV in my tiny room had only three channels, the blanket showed signs of its age, and the small bath towel had good-sized holes in it. Debbie and Sandy said they decided their shower was too grungy to use. However, the village had the good feel of some places on the barrier islands of North Carolina, with neat little shops and good music playing at a *quinceañera* in the nearby town plaza.

We drove back east across the peninsula to the Sea of Cortez, past Loreto, planning to stay overnight in Mulegé.

Postcard views of coves between Loreto and Mulegé at *el Coyote* and *el Burro* enticed us to stop and ask about beachfront palapa residences to rent next winter. We met a retired California husband and wife who live October-May at *el Burro* under a Swiss chalet *palapa* twelve steps across the soft sand from the water's edge. The cove is incredibly beautiful, with warm water for swimming and snorkeling. It has maybe thirty residences, solar power, water from individual storage tanks, and a septic dump station nearby. Each homesite has a ten-year lease purchased for less than $3,000 per year from a local resident who has a concession for the land from the Mexican government. One palapa residence with a house trailer nestled under it was for sale at $37,500 US. Nothing was for rent.

We arrived at Guerrero Negro at lunchtime the next day, changed back to Pacific Time zone at the state line, and headed to *Bahía de los Angeles*, which Sandy visited a year earlier. The little fishing village is about forty miles east of Route 1, with nice views from the mountains of the Sea of Cortez and a few small islands. Electricity arrived in 2007. One guidebook[20] says it is "…the quintessential Baja in the eyes of many." A brochure in a local shop says Jacques Cousteau described the Sea of Cortez there as a natural aquarium.

The best motel in town had rooms for $50 US a night, so we checked in and drove around to see the town before *la cena*. There were many *campos*, some wooden or stone huts for rent, and a few small *casas* for sale; not a prosperous place. Back at the motel, we had the special of grilled fresh shrimp, soup, and salad for eighty pesos.

There was no water in the morning for the sink, shower, or toilet. The manager apologized and told us *un caballo* had broken the water pipe. She showed Debbie how the horse did it, pawing the dirt with her foot. We were skeptical, because Sandy said there was no morning water

---

[20] Ibid, The Baja Adventure Book, p. 138

when she was there a year earlier. She and Debbie took a three-hour guided boat tour of the natural aquarium and said it was great. I was ill again (maybe the salad). The water came back on about 11 a.m., in time for hot showers before we left.

We drove through the mountains on Route 1, past those huge *rocas* and cacti near Cataviña, heading for the Colonet area on the Pacific coast. Sandy and Debbie knew of a little motel/restaurant on the ocean called *la Cueva del Pirata*[21] near Camalu, where they stayed on a previous trip. There was no road sign on Route 1 for it, but we found a bumpy dirt road that looked familiar to them, even in the early evening darkness and a thirty-minute torrential rainstorm. Two or three miles later, after splashing through a truck-sized mudhole, we arrived at the motel. There was so much mud on Sandy's SUV, we laughed that we would not have to worry about being stopped again for an expired registration sticker—nobody could see the license plates.

There were no other overnight guests. Again, there was no water in the morning. The desk clerk apologized and told Debbie that a gravedigger in the nearby cemetery cut the water line accidentally. He didn't show her how it happened. When Debbie saw a water truck arrive to fill the storage tank, the desk clerk changed his story and said a crowd of people at the recent Valentine's Day party used so much water the storage tank ran dry the night we were there. Debbie suggested he could give us *el desayuno gratis* to make up for the lack of water, and he agreed. We headed for home back in La Misión after the free breakfast, through Ensenada, and arrived home by mid afternoon.

The total trip was about 2,200 miles. We split gasoline expenses and paid for food and rooms individually. My total cost for nineteen days was just under 14,000 pesos, less than $1,000 US at that time. That was an average of about $52 per day including gasoline, rooms, meals, and a

---

[21] Pirate's Cove

couple of books. Besides having a great time, I learned a lot about southern Baja (and Debbie and Sandy), including:

– The beaches and mountains are beautiful, and snorkeling and diving and fishing make the area more attractive as an alternative to chilly winter weather in northern Baja. Places on the Sea of Cortez and the East Cape are sometimes fifteen degrees warmer than northern Baja in February. However, residents down south say it is too hot in June-September, with high humidity and temperatures of 100 degrees or more, all the way from Mulegé to Los Cabos.. Like northern Baja, buildings have no heat or air conditioning.

– Much of the area is unspoiled by developers, except for the pricey Los Cabos resort area at the southern tip, but that is changing. Developers already own most private coastal property in southern Baja, or the land is *Ejido* land reserved for agriculture. Available oceanfront lots twenty meters wide range from $50,000 to $800,000 or more, despite the bad economy and shortage of buyers.

– Solar is the primary source of electricity except in towns, with a few small wind turbine generators in backyards on the Pacific coast. Water is scarce, usually from tanker trucks that fill storage tanks of 5,000 gallons or more. We needed our own supply of bottled water, and sometimes we also needed it to bathe. Hot water is rare.

– Septic fields are the norm, except in cities. *Los baños* in public places, restaurants, and Pemex gas stations are unsanitary, frequently without *papel higiénico* and often without water from the sink faucets. We carried our own toilet paper and pocket-size bottles of waterless hand sanitizer.

– Even in nicer motels, flush toilets do not handle toilet paper very well. Some motel room bathrooms have signs in both *español* and *inglés* asking guests to put used *papel higiénico* into a plastic trash bag in the bathroom rather than in the toilet bowl. Other places expect guests to know this custom.

– Fresh *fruta* and *verduras* are plentiful. A good precaution is to rinse fresh fruit and veggies using a solution of bottled water and a few drops of BacDyn®, an iodine-based antiseptic. Or spray the food with a couple of pumps from a handy size bottle of Microcyn®. Using this technique, we bought and enjoyed fresh fruit almost every day, without trouble. I think my two morning bouts of illness were because I didn't obey this basic rule when eating restaurant salads.

– Southern Baja may be safer for residents and travelers. People in all the towns are out after dark. There are far fewer military checkpoints down south than in northern Baja where the military is fighting drug cartels.

During the trip, Debbie and Sandy began talking about buying a RV to travel in southern Baja during winter months, camping on some of those beautiful beaches for $7 to $10 a night. They planned to take their five dogs and maybe their five cats. They invited me to go too, because we traveled well together.

I can see why a lot of *Americanos* and Canadians gravitate to the area in the winter months. However, I don't think traveling in a RV for a month or more is for me.

I Love Baja!

Chapter 17:
Blues, Arts, and Old Farts

San Felipé is a Baja town the tour books say you have to visit. It's on the Sea of Cortez just a couple of hours south of Mexicali and the USA border. For starters, the area has about fifty miles of beaches.

Beach at San Felipé – Debbie Gobe

Mike, a former neighbor of Sandy and Debbie, invited us to join him for a roadtrip to the 3rd Annual Blues & Arts Fiesta in 2009, held at the end of March. The festival was at the city baseball park toward the northern end of town, against a backdrop of mountains and the Sea of Cortez. About thirty booths under sunshades ringed the outfield offering quality original art from local area artists and sculptors. Many were from Rosarito and Ensenada, some were from Arizona and California. The stage and sound system filled the area between home plate and the pitcher's mound. Seating in the bleachers was blocked off, but there was plenty of open space in the sand/dirt/dust infield around the bases for people to dance, or just sit and listen to the music. We realized we would need folding beach chairs and decided to look for them in town after checking out the artists' exhibits.

Many food and beverage booths lined the area between the infield and the outfield. San Felipé is famous for its local *camarones*, and some people say it is the birthplace of the fish taco. Mexican specialties at the fiesta featured $1 tacos of either fish or *camarones,* wrapped in flour or corn tortillas with all the fixings. The smell of cooking tacos, burritos, and enchiladas filled with *carne* or *pollo* filled the air, along with barbecued ribs and chicken.

Women from the Lions club ran the stand that sold food and drink tickets, in addition to souvenirs including T-shirts, bumper stickers, and CDs from bands that were performing free for charity. Men from the Lions club ran the large stand doing a brisk business in cold Tecate beer, bottled water, and soft drinks. After a quick lunch, we drove into the main part of town to find a traditional Mexican open-air *mercado de segunda mano* and bought four folding canvas beach chairs for a total of 300 pesos, or a little over $5 apiece.

Calzada Chetumal is the main road leading to the beach in the heart of the tourist district on the waterfront, and it goes past typical Mexican roadside businesses and shops. Side streets a few blocks from the waterfront are run down and neglected, doors and windows missing, debris on the sidewalks. Between the second and third blocks, we found a parking space for my vehicle with its front and rear body dents and blanket of *polvo*, and nobody bothered it.

Avenue Mar de Cortez, the main street one block back from the waterfront *Malécon*, is lined with shops on both sides selling all sorts of Mexican merchandise and souvenirs. Sandy found loose-fitting summer silk dresses with bold colors, and Debbie found a nice straw hat. We munched on Mexican popsicles in a variety of flavors from a pushcart and strolled along the waterfront.

Bars, restaurants, and cafes, line one side of the *Malécon*, with the public beach and Sea of Cortez on the other side. Mexican families enjoy the beach, sitting under sunshades with picnic coolers, or riding in boats pulling inflatable rafts with seatbelts for four. Sidewalk vendors carry displays of jewelry; some push carts selling tacos or fresh fruit, and others balance three-foot high stacks of straw sombreros on their heads.

For years, the waterfront area of town has been a vacation magnet for spring breakers jamming bars and shops. At low tide, the sixteen-foot tides at San Felipé reveal a huge expanse of shallow sea floor that stretches almost a kilometer into the Sea of Cortez. The exposed beach is great for hordes of beach worshipers enjoying the sand, salt flats, and then the shallow water. We didn't see anyone young enough to be on spring break; maybe warnings from USA officials to avoid Mexico kept the college crowd away. Loudspeakers blared non-stop music anyway from cavernous drinking spots like the Rockodile, complete with a thirty-foot-long green plastic crocodile grinning at us from its perch atop the building.

Back at the festival site, vehicles filled the parking lot, ranging from late model Cadillac and Lincoln SUVs to dune buggies converted from former VWs. License plates were mostly from Arizona, California, Oregon, and Washington. Many were from Rocky Mountain states; a few from Canada; a couple from the Midwest. Clearly, many people from a lot of places in the USA and Canada feel safe visiting or living in San Felipé, despite USA sensationalized news stories about drug violence in Mexico.

Inside the ballpark, vehicles and license plates didn't matter. Tattoos and T-shirts mingled with gold chains and designer tops. Straw hats and wide brims dominated headgear, alongside favorite caps and logos for some of us. The crowd was mostly male and female couples, or groups of friends, as we were.

"It's a combination of blues, arts, and old farts," laughed Mike.

We set our used beach chairs between first and second base, with our backs to the eighty-degree early afternoon sun, and settled in for the afternoon and evening. People filled the infield area, some younger ones crowding the stage to share the performances with others via cell phones. The melting pot ethnic heritage was mostly European, some Latin, a little African, and a little Asian—like a big helping of white rice with chile peppers, spices, and herbs for flavor.

Almost everybody danced now and then. I danced once when a band played a slower song. Some dancers were good, but some were awful, with out-of-sync gyrations. One guy about my age, I think, lost his balance and fell flat on his butt. His dance partner struggled to help him get his aging and overweight body up and back in action.

"It's a little like Woodstock, but forty years and forty pounds later," said Debbie. We lasted until the next-to-last band came on about 8:30 and then decided we had enjoyed enough. One good thing about being older and retired is that people understand if you want to leave early.

Sunday morning, we walked to the poolside cafe on the El Dorado Ranch for the $7.95 champagne brunch. Only two other tables had patrons. Four residents in their seventies sat in wet swimsuits at one table letting it all hang out—women with cover-ups that didn't cover thighs burned brown by the sun; men with no tops to cover big brown bellies. The nearby tennis courts were empty.

I Love Baja!

For decades, the laid-back lifestyle of San Felipé with daytime winter temperatures in the seventies has attracted snowbirds from the USA and Canada. However, winter nighttime lows can be colder than the Pacific coast, dropping into the thirties sometimes. In the summer months, daytime high temperatures can hit 115 or more while the Baja northern Pacific coast is still in the seventy-degree range, and many people avoid the heat in San Felipé. Mike says winds swirl through the desert sometimes and create sandstorms that drive people indoors, much like rainstorms do in parts of the USA. Tour books don't tell you these things.

Over the years, the fishing industry in San Felipé gave way to tourism and then to real estate as people from the USA and Canada headed south. Mike's friends own a home on the manicured golf course meandering through the main El Dorado Ranch village. They use it for rental income, but the most recent entry in the guest book was from June the previous year. Unfinished two-story condos line the golf course, starting right next door. Down the street, the golf clubhouse parking lot had plenty of room, even with the golf special package for only $35, including eighteen holes, a cart, and free use of the practice range.

The El Dorado Ranch straddles the highway for miles, stretching from the Sea of Cortez to the foothills across miles of the desert to the west. Thousands of original homesites remain unsold, and hundreds of lots are for resale at about half the original sales prices of $30,000-$40,000. Several waterfront *campos* remain between the ranch and San Felipé; Pete's Camp on the water's edge has plenty of available spaces starting at $200 US per month. RVs dot the landscape; some occupied, some empty, but not like the large communities of RVs that tour books describe.

On the south edge of town, unfinished condo projects stand empty and deserted. Highway signs offer ocean view and ocean front property in chunks of fifty and sixty acres, and "For Sale" signs stick in the sand in front of sprawling estates ranging from $30,000 to $1.2 million. In the depressed real estate market, some companies are trying to sell one-two bedroom pre-fab houses at prices between $35,000-$70,000. Buyers can choose from several designs, stucco house trailers essentially, with Spanish architectural facades. Put some money down, truck the house to your lot somewhere out there in desert, and plug it into the electrical grid. Of course, you need to hire another truck to haul water to refill your *pila* now and then, and you need to install your own septic system. Nevertheless, for less than $100,000 including land, you can live in a place that is like the Arizona desert, but with an endless beach and enormous tides.

Mike would like to build something someday on his building lot and spend winters in the desert rather than in the golf community where he lives just south of Ensenada. During the trip, we went to his site four miles into the desert from the highway, past a two-level observation post that simulated what a rooftop view would be. We could see almost forever, all the way to the Sea of Cortez and back to the mountains.

However, building a home in the San Felipé area is not cheap - about $100 a square foot - because contractors have to truck all building materials almost 100 miles from somewhere like the Mexicali urban area. Some expatriates say the cold desert winter nights and hot summer days boost the energy bills to an average of $250-300 monthly.

To reduce construction and energy costs, some people are building eco-friendly dwellings with thick walls, and using hand-made adobe bricks and trying solar and wind for alternative energy. Others are building "tire houses" using junkyard tires packed with desert dirt, stacked on top of each other, and then covered with stucco. We stopped and took pictures of a good-looking yellow tire house, with two master bedrooms, advertised for sale at $169,000 by the artist who designed it. One resident has a tire house partially underground covered with an earthen berm.

Tire House and Wall near San Felipé – Debbie Gobe

The real estate industry has changed San Felipé at least twice—once during the boom, now during the bust. Maybe the area will change again in a few years, when USA and Canadian retirees scramble to find an affordable and safe retirement place where the winters are warmer. In the meantime, some local realty offices have closed. Developers and other realtors sit tight in the San Felipé sun waiting for the economy to recover and for drug violence along the USA-Mexican border to diminish.

It's hard to describe San Felipé in a short summary paragraph because it offers so much. However, I concluded that the tour books are correct. It's great place, with great beaches, a good waterfront *Malécon,* and a comfortable multi-cultural atmosphere. The Blues & Arts Fiesta is great fun, and I began planning to go back for the 4th annual event in March of 2010. It's not my ideal retirement place, however, at least not year-round. Blowing desert sand, cold winter nights, high summer heat, and high energy costs all year are big negatives for me.

In the spring of 2009, Baja Burgers did not reopen. Jesse and Rosa were at the annual rodeo and folkloric festival in La Misión a month or so later and we chatted briefly. They were living nearby, but were unsure if they would open the cafe again. They looked okay but were hesitant to talk. Their smiles were strained.

Sometime in the late summer, word spread that they were open again and I went to find them. The new location was close to *el granero*, but smaller than the fall before. It was perched on the edge of the hill overlooking the river valley, stuck up against the wall of a neighboring building, with the other three sides open to the elements. The dirt parking area had room for only a couple cars, barely big enough me to park without sticking out onto Route 1.

Only two small white plastic tables remained, each with two red plastic chairs. The kitchen refrigerator nestled against the wire mesh wall overlooking the valley. A deep fryer sat against the building wall, alongside a substantial homemade open grill with glowing charcoal. Jesse welcomed me with a broad smile from behind the narrow table he used as a counter.

"The menu's not the same," he said, apologizing. The top-of-the-line Baja Burger combo was *no mas*, he said; just a regular quarter-pound cheeseburger with a packaged Bimbo bun. Moreover, the *papas fritas* were precut, in frozen packages from the store. However, it had all the fixings, and came with a cold *Coca Zero*® in a can, for just forty pesos.

"*No hay problema*," I said, practicing my best *español* accent. "I'm just happy to see you."

I asked about Rosa, with the smile and the dimples. He said she was working sometimes at Magaña's restaurant, the one with the cowboy bar and hitching post for *caballos*, down the hill by the bridge over the river.

When I returned for a takeout combo a couple of weeks later, just before closing time, Rosa was sitting at one of the tables. She smiled and her dimples crinkled at me again. Her son was sitting at the table with her, doing more homework. I recalled the saying they had painted on the beam of the little cafe when it was up the hill back in 2008 —"Free Burgers *Mañana.*" We all laughed.

They're going to make it, I thought to myself as I left. But I was wrong. *En octubre*, the iron gate was shut and padlocked. It was still padlocked *en noviembre.* At *el granero* next door, *la senora* shook her head sadly when I asked what happened.

"*Ya no está,*"[22] she said sadly.

"*No mas?*" I asked, not understanding exactly what she said.

"*Si, no mas,*" she replied.

---

[22] It's gone.

I Love Baja!

Chapter 18:

Roadhouses and Cafes

Standalone roadhouses and cafes on the side of the Route 1 have been an essential ingredient in the flavor of Baja for decades.

Some authentic roadhouses have been around since way back when and have a distinctive well-worn look. Other restaurants and little cafes are newer, more like replicas you might find in USA suburbs. Newer expatriates own some of them, looking for a slice of the economic pie in Baja.

On the Baja Gold Coast between Rosarito and Ensenada, roadhouses and cafes include the Half Way House at Medio Camino, Splash, La Salina Cantina, La Fonda, Poco Cielo, Magañas, La Bamba, Bobby's-By-The-Sea, Ricky's Place, Joanna's *Galeria y Café,* and Ruben's Palm Grill. The 2008 economic collapse makes business harder for all of them, but each has a loyal clientele of expatriate regulars who live nearby and are frequent customers.

The Half Way House is a treasured historic landmark —halfway between Tijuana and Ensenada beside the ocean at Km53 on the free road—the first roadhouse between the two towns. It has a plaque on the outside wall dating it to 1922.

Niemann's book "*Baja Legends*" features its past. It also hosts a pit stop for thousands of amateur cyclists on the annual fifty-mile spring and fall bicycle rides from Rosarito to Ensenada.

Rosarito-Ensenada Bike Riders at the Half Way House

The real treasure is Juan Ramon (Chef Johnny), a warm huggy-bear in a chef's tunic, who trained in classical French cuisine in San Francisco and was a traveling chef for the President of Mexico. If you guarantee reservations for six to ten people, he and his wife Julia will prepare a multi-course gourmet French meal matched with L.A. Cetto wines, all for about $30 per person. The food alone would cost more than three times as much a la carte in San Francisco. After dinner, he might strum his Spanish guitar or sing something from Italian opera as you sit by the fireplace and look at the sunset over the Pacific. There is nothing better.

Splash is a newer place not far from the Half Way House. It's named for the big splash when the ocean crashes onto the lava flow cliff just fifty feet from the outdoor dining area. Locals know to arrive early to get a front row table with a great view. Nicholas and his brother Agapo took over the business in early 2010, bringing stability to the service and the kitchen. Now the great menu features fresh seafood dishes, with service as satisfying as watching the ocean splash twenty feet into the air. Very good lobster bisque, even fried oysters. They put up a palapa outside and expanded the inside to include a bar with a dance floor and a little stage for live entertainment. It became THE place to be. Smoke and smokers sometimes fill the bar, separate from the dining room. Still, you have to love a place with an assistant bartender named Lolita.

La Salina Cantina overlooks a wide sandy beach next to the Puerto Salina Marina. The menu and service are good enough, and the jukebox has *gringo* favorites. A backroom pool table area ignores the Mexican ban on smoking indoors. Jesse, the main bartender, has that irresistible Mexican charm that causes many aging *gringas* to sit and chat. A big attraction is getting something from the bar and sipping it as you walk along the beach and wade in the surf at sunset. The place never was the same after developers took over the beach in the fall of 2009 and blocked beach access with posts and barbed wire and a plywood guard shack. It infuriated regulars. They couldn't do anything about it except squeeze between the barbed wire strands to get to the beach after the guard left at the end of the day. To retaliate, they started hitting golf balls at the shack and him from a makeshift tee area on the cantina patio.

The iconic La Fonda restaurant and inn is located near the Km63 exit on the toll road, sitting on a slender strip of clifftop on Route 1 above the ocean. There is just enough space for a few restaurants, hotels, and stores squeezed together side by side. For years and years, the beach in this area has been a prized getaway for people from the states, with La Fonda as the centerpiece.

Pacific Ocean, Looking South from La Fonda

Locals say Dimitri, the former owner, met everyone at the restaurant door, charmed the ladies and offered them free drinks, and schmoozed with guests at the tables. La Fonda's new owners try to keep the ambiance while making the bar-restaurant-inn-spa more hip. At the L-shaped bar, sports fans keep up with football and basketball in the USA or with *fútbol* around the globe. *Turistas* in designer jeans and surfers in cutoffs share space on the hardwood floor in the outdoor dining room on seasonal weekends, enjoying live music from decent dance bands.

Small wood-burning fireplaces in the restaurant beckon diners to snuggle up next to the flickering flames and glowing embers in cooler months. A small chalkboard outside the open front doors has the scrawled invitation Dimitri made famous: "Sit your wonderful selves anyplace." It's still a back-in-time oasis, but many people miss his charm. Even without Dimitri, it's more than just a place to eat, drink, or stay. It's more like visiting *una mujer lindísima* who always has a warm welcome for you. You want to see her again soon, snuggle up to a little fireplace, and savor another cup of *café Mexicano*.

Poco Cielo is a cozy little restaurant and inn next door to La Fonda. It has a big fireplace on the open-air dining level, and stairs that tumble down the cliff to the beach below. Cheryl, the feisty owner, keeps trying to improve the tasty dishes on the menu and out-do whatever La Fonda is doing. First it was her 99-cent Margaritas. Then she stuck up a new highway sign so big it almost obscured the La Fonda sign. In 2009 she added a huge oceanfront patio next door, big enough to host the organic market twice a month. In 2010 she added a big indoor bar with a dance floor and live entertainment. I wouldn't bet against her.

Magañas is a neat little family cafe by the bridge at the river in La Misión, with a big plywood roadside sign always saying it's for sale. The dining room features condiment bowls of roasted red and green peppers, with green onions grilled until they're almost black. It also has a killer carrot cake and a whole *pollo rotisada* that even Mexicans buy and take home to eat. It's one of my favorite take-out meals, too. The place also has a real cowboy cantina added onto the side next to the river, with a long wooden hitching post out back for *caballos* and a backdoor entrance for *vaqueros*. At the end of the week, cowboys from ranches in the hills up the river fill the little cantina with jukebox music, cigarette smoke, and laughter. The bartender explained one time how the *vaqueros* could find their way back to the ranches in the dark after a few hours at the cantina.

"The horses, they know the way, *no?*" he said.

La Bamba is a newer retro-fifties roadside diner closer to the downtown area of Rosarito. You know you've found La Bamba when you see the front end of a yellow Chevy pickup hanging over the entrance to a roadside building. The overall paint scheme is red and white and black, inside and out, with fifties' stuff for decorations. A jukebox in the corner plays songs of lost California youth. Whatever patrons feel like writing covers the back wall from top to bottom, side to side. A big picture of the Hollywood "Rat Pack" shooting pool is on another wall. Pictures of James Dean, Mickey Mantle, and other male icons hang alongside. A poster of Lucy and her famous Vita-meta-vega-min commercial is on one wall. The men's room has a couple of pictures of Marilyn Monroe in provocative poses, one of which proves she was a brunette. Really.

La Bamba Cafe, Rosarito

The menu features homemade biscuits on a par with the best in the USA, favorites such as chicken-fried steak, and burgers hundreds of ways with scrumptious sides. Susan's special desserts include fresh fruit pies and cobblers (try the strawberry pie), and banana walnut fudge ice cream cones. The full bar menu offers specialty drinks and "less-milk-more-shake" malts with alcohol. You can order takeout meals of weekly specials and to-die-for desserts. La Bamba. A big helping of California from the fifties, right here in Baja.

Bobby's-By-The-Sea is an *Americano* restaurant near Puerto Nuevo that sprouted a couple of ostentatious faded-yellow mid-rise condo towers. Some people say the bar has one of the best Bloody Marys on the Baja Gold Coast. The restaurant has pretty good food, especially the corned beef and cabbage Bobby makes to celebrate St. Patrick's Day. The balding, gruff-talking, New York refugee presiding over everything is Bobby. Poker is his game and horse racing is his passion, with TV sets in the bar showing coverage of tracks around North America. Don't bet against him on ANYthing.

Ricky's Place perches on the ocean on the sweeping curve just south of Calafia, next to a couple of places not good enough to mention. A sign on the front has a picture of Enrique in his trademark Stetson with the wide brim turned up like big ears. A row of sandbags guards the front door to divert the downhill runoff in case it rains. The barroom is about as dark as a bar can get. It takes a moment for your eyes to adjust before you can see the main attraction—a pole smack in the center of the barroom for wannabe pole dancers. Ricky calls it the "woo-woo" pole, named for the "WOO! WOO! WOO!" chant patrons used to shout while encouraging spring break coeds and other vacationing *gringas* to bare their breasts. He says he was amazed at how many responded to the chants—a Baja version of "Girls Gone Wild." Dozens of bras hang on the walls, mementos of the days before the USA warned college students not to travel to Mexico and before the economy crashed.

The place gained fame briefly while Russell Crowe was filming "Master and Commander" at the nearby Fox oceanfront studios. He and other cast members partied there often, according to locals, and kept the place jumping way past midnight. Now the bar and the well-worn dance floor around the pole are almost empty most nights. Behind the main barroom area is a small dining room, with a couple of outdoor tables and chairs beyond that. A few locals sip Margaritas or *cervezas*, nibble on appetizers, and ignore Mexico's ban on smoking in public places. Ricky in his hat tries to get them to stay for dinner.

Food never was the real attraction.

Joanna's *Galeria y Café* is unlike any of the other places—no bicycle riders or pictures of movie stars, no jukebox or ocean view, no TVs for sports fans, no cowboys or horses, and no pole on the dance floor. It's between Puerto Nuevo and Cantamar on Route 1, open only on Friday, Saturday, and Sunday from 12-5 p.m., or maybe later if enough people want to stay. The *galeria* is a narrow three-story Victorian replica painted pink and blue, peeking out between palm trees, crammed with art and books and crafts that overflow some days into the parking spaces. The café is stuck onto the backside - just a tiny space under a thatched palapa roof - with a fridge and a stove and three bar stools. The little patio has a couple of high tables with some bar chairs and a few more sitting chairs under an impressive canopy of bougainvillea vines.

Joanna's Galeria y Café near Cantamar

If you linger long enough, other expatriates trickle in and out, thirsty for intellectual conversation and the wines Joanna serves from the *Valle de Guadalupe*. She also imports genuine 100 percent Kona coffee from Hawaii and uses a

French press to fill your cup twice for $1.50 US. She offers organic cheeses from the valley to complement fresh fruit in season, with olives and crackers on the side. Sometimes the cheese maker lingers also, describing the art of producing delicate flavors and aromas and asking patrons how much to charge *turistas* in the wine country.

It doesn't have what some other places have. It doesn't have the business that it once had, back when people came for poetry readings and wine tastings and classical guitar music. In October 2010, it became the site for the resurrected annual Baja Book Festival featuring authors, artists, food, wine, beer, tequila, and music. And it has Joanna, with a quick laugh and smiling eyes the color of jade, filled with a passion for Tango.

Ruben's Palm Grill is a survivor, taking over a failed restaurant at the Cantamar exit near Joanna's. After moving from his location on Route 1 across from Las Gavitos, Ruben moved to prime real estate right at the Cantamar exit on the toll road. The ambitious menu aims to please expats rather than Mexicans. He spiffed up the building with its huge palapa roof, added some summertime seating under thatched roofs, a playground for kids, and specials almost every night of the week. Plus music at least four nights a week. So far, so good.

There are many other hangouts, some big and some small, some doing well and some struggling to survive the economic collapse and fears of drug cartel violence in border cities. Longtime legends prosper at opposite ends of the Baja Gold Coast—Hussong's Cantina in Ensenada opened in 1892, and El Rey Sol with its five-star French cuisine opened in 1947. The Rosarito Beach Hotel and its opulent Chabert's restaurant in downtown Rosarito dates to 1925. El Nido in downtown Rosarito has survived since 1970 by offering Mexican specialties in addition to locally-grown venison, lamb, rabbit, and quail cooked over mesquite firewood. The family raises 250,000 of its own quails every year on their own farms.

Nearby, Susanna's relatively new upscale restaurant with an extensive wine cellar targets tourists with its "cuisine of the Californias" and struggles to find a successful niche despite the perky persona of Susanne in her cowboy boots and ponytail. The down-scale No Bad Days sports bar has had better days, despite Lyn's secret recipe for a Bloody Mary and Jim's genuine antique coin-operated shuffleboard table that attracts the faithful few.

Small taco stands are able to survive better than most other food places. Taco places are everywhere, serving the Mexican staple for ten pesos and up. My favorite is Sandra's little taco cart next to Paco's Market at Km58 on Route 1, on the city limits between Rosarito and Ensenada. She tows it to her spot every morning, offering fish tacos for ten pesos and shrimp tacos for fifteen pesos. Customers add toppings from the various sauces, shredded lettuce and onions, and *pico de gallo*.

Sandra's Taco Cart on Route 1 at Km58

One of the better-known *taqueros* is Tacos el Yaqui, a block off the main street in downtown Rosarito. It's been around for twenty years or so, according to locals. Both *Vogue* and *Condé Nast* mentioned it several years ago. The owners also operate El Gerente down the street two blocks away. The kitchen staff there sometimes amuses patrons by talking loudly about cutting up *perros y gatos,* then making sounds of dogs and cats yelping in pain. Helanne says it was unnerving the first time she heard it.

In downtown Rosarito, trendy giant joints such as Iggy's and Papas & Beer once ruled the main boulevard; they struggled after drug cartel violence decimated the throngs. Alice and Lynnsie, two fellow writers, say as many as 5,000 *Americano*s would pay $25 each to drink and dance to loud music until 5 a.m., but *no mas.*

In early summer 2010, a sports bar named *Que Paso?* opened amid the newer places on the northern edge of Rosarito close to Home Depot, Wal-Mart, and the cineplex. Detroit native Tim and his Mexican wife Olga feature hamburgers and hot dogs cooked on a charcoal grill outside the back door. In the fall, owners at Bahia Cantiles took over the nearby El Pescador and rebranded it as "Fiesta at El Pescador." Now it features Texas-style barbecue, an outdoor palapa, a large private banquet room, and a dance band that tries to attract enough people to fill the big hardwood floor. In early 2011, East Coast refugee Richard opened a dine-in gourmet pizza place near Las Gaviotas and named it after his dog Ollie. His wood-fired oven turns out special-recipe pizzas equal to the best in the USA with fresh ingredients—nothing from a can or a jar or a box.

It's always a good idea to check to see if a place is still open before making plans to meet there with someone. Some small places couldn't survive the combination of economic free fall and fears about drug cartel violence. Dennis, an American writer who owned Diego's Deli, closed his little shop at Thanksgiving in 2009 and returned to Ohio right after the last batch of pumpkin pies. Fuku, a pricey

Japanese sushi place not far from La Bamba, closed and the Japanese owners disappeared. Longtime stalwart Rene's Sports Bar just locked the doors. So did La Palapa de Jose at the K-58 campground.

Now and then minor events detract from the local charm of some places. As a precaution, I learned the value of reading menus *en español* and calculating the exchange rate between pesos and U.S. dollars. I wouldn't want to accuse some places of deliberately ripping off customers. Nonetheless, misunderstandings arise sometimes over the amount of the bill or *el cambio* after paying the bill. This usually happens when several people are in a group. The bill might have different charges than the menu prices, maybe a few extra drinks, some food that people didn't order, or an unfavorable exchange rate. Some places charge *gringos* more for food and drinks, discounting the price for Mexicans.

Rosella taught me a valuable phrase to use in any financial transaction in Baja, especially at restaurants: *"cuentas claras, amistades largas"*—when the count is clear, friendships are long. It isn't always effective. One time it didn't work was at a popular restaurant/cantina during a crowded night for a televised pay-per-view championship fight. Fred and Idalia were with me, and all of us were sure I gave the waiter a 500-peso bill. But the waiter brought back change for a 200-peso bill, and he and the bartender refused to return my correct *cambio*. My friendship didn't last very long with that place.

Some of my friends rave now and then about eating in four-star restaurants in San Diego, Tijuana, or Ensenada. Over time I developed my own rating system for roadhouses and cafes in Baja.

They get one star if they have soap and water for employees to wash hands; otherwise, I don't eat there.

A second star is for good food and drinks at fair prices. A third star is for good service and honest waiters, waitresses, and bartenders. A fourth star is for overall cleanliness and atmosphere, with maybe a good view.

All the places mentioned in my book rate at least three of my stars, even Sandra's taco cart, where she washes her hands with soap and *agua purificada* before preparing each taco.

Except for Iggy's.

I went to Iggy's one time, during the 2010 annual Baja Sand Sculpture event. Debbie, Sandy, Vickie, Millie, April, Lupita and two of her kids and some friends of the kids wanted to sit in the shade on the beach and sip something cool. It turned out the inviting chairs crowded under a little palapa belonged to Iggy's, and it cost $7 for each Margarita when the waiter brought the bill.

That offended Lupita, because the Margaritas were supposed to be two for $6 that afternoon. She figured the waiter got a glimpse of Millie's diamond ear studs and saw opportunity. So she had words with him in animated *español*. I think the waiter tried to claim the $6 was the minimum charge, even if people had just one Margarita, and the extra dollar was for the tip, but I'm not certain. Whatever...Lupita wasn't happy.

Cuentas claras, amistades largas. Maybe that's another reason Iggy's doesn't have as many customers as before.

They get two stars.

I Love Baja!

Chapter 19:
Baja Brownies

Almost everybody in northern Baja has at least one funny story about crossing the border between the USA and Mexico. One of the funniest is the one Tim tells about a U.S. retiree who likes to buy American rather than buying in Mexico, if you know what I mean.

It adds to the story if you can visualize the guy in the story—let's call him "Joe." He has a big-belly-laugh, and he usually wears a T-shirt, shorts, and sandals. He refuses to wear a hat, so his forehead is sunburned to the same reddish color as his face, and it gets redder when he is spinning yarns and sipping Margaritas on his patio. He has been visiting Baja since he was four years old and loves the place. After taking a disability retirement, he moved to Baja to live in a dream house overlooking the Pacific Ocean with his longtime live-in girlfriend.

In case you miss the obvious, Tim says, Joe gets some homegrown stuff now and then from friends back in California. It's less risky that way, and he trusts them to control the quality. He may be one of the few people who bring marijuana into Mexico.

The way Tim tells the story, Joe was coming down the I-5 south of San Diego one day with some potted ornamental bushes for his new *casa*. Like most experienced drivers coming into Mexico, he steered clear of the *"Declaraciõn"* lanes at the border for Mexican customs. However, he never thought about a few potted plants being illegal.

Anybody at the border checkpoint could see Joe had live plants in the back of his pickup truck, leaves and branches fluttering in the breeze. Sure enough, the Mexican *policia* "red lighted" him and blocked him from entering Mexico. Then they herded his pickup through an opening in the steel border fence that separates *Bienvenido* from *Adios*.

A big steel gate slammed shut behind him as he completed the forced U-turn. Now he was in a checkpoint area controlled by U.S. Customs and Border Patrol (CBP) agents, because he was headed back into the USA.

Tim says a CBP agent told Joe he couldn't take potted plants from Mexico across the border, and he started big-belly-laughing at the absurdity of the situation. How could he be taking the plants out of Mexico if authorities blocked him from taking the same plants into Mexico just a few minutes earlier?

The agent didn't laugh, and she wanted to check inside the pickup.

Joe realized this could be trouble, because he had some homegrown California pot in a small plastic bag, tucked inside a folded newspaper in a briefcase. But, what could he do?

He flipped the switch to unlock the doors, and suddenly a sniffer dog with an attitude was in the front seat with him. The dog was sticking its nose everywhere, sniffing and panting like border dogs do. It was poking around by his sandals, sniffing his bare legs, and slobbering on his bare ankles and toes.

"What's in the briefcase?" the agent asked. "Open it."

Joe knew he was in REALLY BIG trouble. His heart was pounding, and all he could do was say okay.

Tim says the dog sniffed and drooled all over the folded newspaper. Apparently it didn't pick up the scent of what was right under its nose. An Agriculture Inspector intervened about then to look at the plants, and the CBP agent yanked the dog out of the cab. The Ag inspector discussed the potted plants, scribbled some notes on an official form, gave Joe a copy, and let him across the border.

Joe took the I-5 north, dropped the plants at a buddy's house, spent the night, and headed back to Mexico the next morning. He honked and waved at the Mexican *policia* at the border, then drove right past them with the same briefcase and all its contents. I was laughing uncontrollably by then, because Tim is a great storyteller.

I was curious about why the dog didn't pick up the scent of the guy's stash. According to Tim, maybe the dog was trained to smell cocaine. Or, he says Joe told him, maybe the dog had never smelled anything as good as the homegrown stuff from the USA.

"Joe" verified the story for me, although he says Tim elaborated just a bit.

On August 21, 2009, Mexico decriminalized possessing less than five grams of marijuana for personal use. Right away, "Boomer" decided to try pot, now that it was less likely he would get arrested. It makes an amusing little story, told with the naivete of someone who was too scared to use pot back in the USA.

He says his first experience with Mexican pot was sharing a joint, and most of his friends in Baja were stunned to learn that he had never tried marijuana. They tried to help him avoid coughing and coached him on what to do.

"Not too much," he says they told him. "Hold it in. Now, let it out slowly." He says the high began in a few minutes and lasted about two hours.

Boomer's next hits were from a pipe people passed around at a neighborhood party. The pipe wouldn't stay lit, and he says he kept burning his thumbnail with the lighter flame. He managed to inhale enough to make him seem funnier than usual, and told people at the party he might tell others about the experience. He says they laughed and told him everybody else already knew what it was like.

In northern Baja, apparently, part of the marijuana culture involves the price difference between marijuana sold in the USA and the stuff Mexicans call *mota*. According to Boomer, some users in Baja say high quality USA-grown marijuana retails for around $400 per ounce in Southern California. Some serious users say they pay $500 an ounce for really good pot grown in the USA. Boomer says other users tell him the asking price for Mexican *mota* in northern Baja is just $40, with plenty available at $25 per ounce.

Boomer couldn't tell if the USA stuff in the pipe at the party was any better than the Mexican joint. So, a couple of weeks later, he arranged a little focus group of friends to test Mexican pot. He gave $25 to a user friend to add an ounce of it to a box of Ghirardelli chocolate fudge brownie mix. All the friends had experiences with other marijuana in other places, he says.

One person was at Woodstock. A second smoked pot once in an Amsterdam cannabis cafe, and said he had trouble finding his hotel for a couple of hours afterward.

A third smoked her first joint in high school. She admitted to smoking a lot more in her twenties while riding bare-breasted on the back of her boyfriend's motorcycle.

A fourth confided that she did a full Lady Godiva at a hometown parade back in Oregon after borrowing a horse from a friend in the sheriff's mounted posse. Her pipe was the one Boomer couldn't keep lit.

"There may be truth in a bottle of wine," says Boomer, "But you never really know your friends until you invite them to share some pot."

The 8x8 glass baking pan produced brownies an inch thick. The baker cut them into sixteen 2x2 squares, each with slightly less pot than two medium-size joints. They started watching a DVD movie and nibbling the brownies.

"Ghirardelli makes great chocolate fudge brownies, and I ate the whole thing," says Boomer. He started feeling the effects in about an hour and had wobbly legs, like after taking Xanax® or Valium® for an airplane flight.

"Everything began moving in slow motion and I couldn't feel the pavement while I was walking home," he says. "I was wide awake and still flying high at 5:30 a.m."

Most of the others told him a few days later that they had similar experiences. Apparently, based on Boomer's focus group, Mexican pot is good—or good enough.

I'm not suggesting people should try marijuana, or that people should never try it. Those are individual choices. Most people I know are aware that some studies show it contains carcinogens, just like tobacco products. In addition, some U.S. authorities still insist that marijuana is a gateway drug that leads to other drug use.

Boomer says one of his friends in Baja laughs at that.

"The only drug it leads to is Viagra® to help you follow up on those mellow feelings," his friend told him.

Actually, headlines in the USA and around the world were misleading about Mexico legalizing marijuana. According to legal analyses of the new law, what Mexico did was designed to rehabilitate users and provide government-funded help in treatment centers. Maybe, maybe not. Legal analysts say that under the new law, if you have only five grams in your possession and authorities catch you, they will issue a written warning and not arrest you as a criminal. If you receive *trés advertencias*, the new law considers you an *adicto* and requires you to go into a mandatory rehabilitation program. Still, it is a significant milestone that Mexico decriminalized possession of less than five grams of marijuana for personal use.

That means Boomer was an outlaw, however, because his batch of Baja brownies with an ounce of pot equaled twenty-eight grams. He says he could imagine *la policia* knocking on his door and asking him, *"Que pasa, señor?"*

YOU IDIOT, he realized. YOU ARE IN MEXICO, where possession of more than the new limit STILL means mandatory time in a nasty Mexican jail for at least a few days, maybe weeks, or months.

So, after his three marijuana experiences and understanding the new Mexican law better, Boomer decided to just say no. No more shared joints, puffs from a party pipe, or yummy brownies for dessert. *No mas. Nada.* He figured he would sleep better, both literally and figuratively.

Boomer decided to implement his new policy in a week or two, right after he got rid of the rest of those leftover brownies in his freezer. He gave some of them away to other friends, a couple at a time in plastic baggies, being careful not to carry more than the new legal limit. He explained what they were and urged his friends to be careful.

Almost five weeks later, one of Boomer's friends returned home after a morning meeting and found his wife sitting in her favorite armchair, holding onto both arms and staring off into space. She told her husband she felt really strange and said her mind was doing weird things. The husband, a retired physician, checked her vital signs and asked her if she had eaten anything unusual.

"Just a leftover brownie I found in the fridge," his wife replied. Uh-oh—the husband had not cautioned her about the brownies.

The husband told Boomer the brownies didn't do much for him, and that's why there were still a couple in the fridge five weeks later.

"They certainly did something for my wife," he said. "And it took so long for her to come down, we almost missed a dinner party."

Chapter 20:
Lower Your Pants, *Señor*

In the fall of 2008 I began using local doctors and dentists in Baja almost exclusively. In 2009 I began buying all my medicine in Baja. Paying cash in Baja for doctors and medicine was not much more expensive than the co-pay for my U.S. group insurance coverage. Why go back to the USA?

My first glimpse of health care in Mexico was in January 2006, courtesy of my cousin Hope. I was impressed. She needed a mouthful of dental work and had researched medical tourism options on the Internet to find something cheaper than where she lived in Missouri. She found a reputable *dentista* in Tijuana and a rental place in Rosarito for a month-long vacation. I was planning my first trip to La Misión, the vacation trip that launched my Baja journey.

A couple of days after settling into our respective places, I drove Hope to the Pacific Dental office in the Zona Rio section of Tijuana. It was as nice as my family dentist's office back in Maryland. One of the dentists gave us a tour of the state-of-the-art equipment, including digital imaging rather than X-rays—more advanced than my dentist office— and plenty of new equipment for sterilizing dental tools.

Both dentists were probably in their early thirties, educated and board certified in San Diego. They had their own dental lab onsite, just across the hallway—no week or two delay to send out impressions and wait for crowns or dentures.

During Hope's initial two-hour procedure, I chatted with patients coming and going in the waiting room. One woman had driven her mother down from San Diego—just a three-hour round trip including treatment. Another said she had been a Hollywood body double for Jamie Lee Curtis in a couple of movies. A couple in their seventies was from Utah, staying at San Diego motel. No one was concerned about the quality of Mexican dental care or afraid to be in Tijuana.

Hope made several more visits to the *dentista* while I was in Baja for those two weeks and almost finished everything before I returned to Maryland. She told me the umpteen crowns and whatever else cost about half what she would have paid in rural Missouri—the cost per crown was less than one-third what I paid in Maryland.

My next experience with Mexican medical care was firsthand. I tripped while going up steps to my little apartment in early evening darkness, my arms full of groceries, and I banged my forehead on a corner of the concrete wall. It almost knocked me out. Blood ran down my face from the gash on the top edge of my right eyebrow. I cleaned the wound with my first aid kit, stopped the bleeding, stuck on a bandage, and drove to Ensenada the next morning for follow-up treatment.

The receptionist at the private Velmar Hospital understood perfectly what I needed and directed me to an office on the third floor. The assistant said *el doctor* would see me shortly. In about ten minutes, he came to get me, walked me back to an examining room, and determined quickly what to do.

He took me to an ER room and, with an assistant, spent about fifteen minutes cleaning the wound more thoroughly and applying a topical antibiotic. They took some

I Love Baja!

X-rays to make certain I hadn't damaged a sinus cavity. They glued the wound shut and stuck on a couple of butterfly bandages to hold it together for a few days. We discussed *en inglés* whether I wanted plastic surgery later, and I said no, because the inch-long scar would not be very noticeable. He sent me to the hospital pharmacy for a prescription oral antibiotic, and told me to pay the cashier for everything. The total bill, including the prescription, was less than $50 US. One of my friends said later that was higher than some other places.

For a cold that turned into bronchial pneumonia, I used a walk-in local *clinica* in La Misión and it was fine. *El medico* charged just 100 pesos for the office visit and a shot of antibiotics, about half of my co-pay back in the USA for a similar visit to a walk-in medical service. The difference in Baja was that a young *señorita,* the assistant to *el médico*, administered the shot of antibiotics.

"*Por favor*, lower your pants, *señor*," she told me. I loved her Spanish accent and joked that they could have charged *mucho mas*. As I was paying the bill, I offered her a ten-peso *propina*, but she just laughed and declined.

Other expatriates and Mexican citizens in Baja told me of still less expensive visits to *dentistas* and *médicos*. Many health care providers see patients in small offices scattered along primary roads or in homes. Elizabeth, a Polish poet, had a tooth extracted for only $20 after the writers workshop luncheon one week and I agreed to drive her home afterward. She said *la dentista* told her to use Tequila as both a painkiller and substitute for antibiotics.

I told her that might be stretching the limits of alternative medicine, and maybe the word "antibiotics" suffered in translation from English to Spanish to Polish and back to English. But she was certain and bought two bottles of Tequila on the way home, for medicinal use.

Some *médicos* treat the Mexican working poor for even less, or provide free treatment to those without income. At one *farmacia* in downtown Rosarito, an onsite *médico* charges just twenty pesos before recommending what medicines to buy. Down in La Misión, a *médico* and his *esposa* serve the poor for free from their two-room home, and she helps coordinate a volunteer food bank. I donated some beans and a 100-pound sack of rice (*frijoles y arroz*).

Emergency medical attention in Baja is easy to obtain and relatively inexpensive. *Cruz Roja* runs all the emergency services, including the *ambulancia* service, and funds its operations mostly from volunteer donations, with fees for some services. Their offices up and down the main highways are open from 9 a.m. - 9 p.m., Monday-Saturday, and you can walk in for ambulatory first aid attention. Or, if you are unable to get there yourself, just enter 066 from any cell phone or landline, explain the situation *en inglés*, and they will dispatch the appropriate medical personnel.

When my neighbor Debbie broke her ankle in the spring of 2008, emergency responders gave her first aid on the hillside where she fell while walking her dogs back from the beach. The *ambulancia* then took her to the *Cruz Roja* medical center in the center of Rosarito Beach, twenty miles toward the border, where she received an X-ray diagnosis and a temporary cast. All of it cost about $50, including the cost of the *ambulancia* ride.

The *Cruz Roja ambulancia* would have taken her all the way to the USA border, but she rode with friends to her HMO facility in San Diego for extensive surgery and a few days of follow-up care to repair the severely broken ankle. Other friends told me later they once paid $200 US for the 17-mile *ambulancia* ride to the border and had to pay in cash upfront.

Sandy and Debbie, both of them pre-Medicare age, decided in 2009 to check out the Mexican national health care system available through the Mexican Institute of Social Security (IMSS).[23] Sandy had heard good comments from an expat

---

[23] Mexico Living, October 2009, p. 10

friend who enrolled in IMSS. She seemed determined to try it and perhaps discontinue her U.S. coverage with its high monthly premiums. Maybe the best way to get the facts was to go with them to the IMSS central office in Tijuana and discuss coverage with a program official.

To facilitate conversations, Debbie enlisted her good friend Lupita from Tijuana to go with us, because she and her four children were IMSS participants. It took two trips to IMSS facility No. 7 in the central part of town just to understand how to apply. Both trips were experiences in Mexican bureaucratic efficiency, much like in the USA.

The IMSS complex occupies most of two city blocks and includes medical offices, medical personnel, and administrative personnel. Cars jam the cross streets near the complex, drivers jockeying around double-parked vehicles and vendors with vans and street carts. Building entrances have lines of people waiting to get inside where there are more lines. At the first building entrance, we received a spray of antiseptic on our hands from a bottle wielded by a worker standing in the doorway. I was impressed until I went to *el baño* and discovered no running water, soap, or towels. *No hay problema*—I learned long ago to carry a pocket-sized waterless hand sanitizer.

After two more entrances and two more sprays, we found an information desk around the corner and down the block with someone who could answer questions from Lupita about how to apply. The first step would be to come back a week later to participate in a general information session for new applicants. We left the building and took Lupita to her favorite restaurant for *la comida* to celebrate our success.

On the second trip we headed straight for the proper entrance, received our antiseptic spray, and went up the stairs to the auditorium for the information meeting. A friendly worker outside the room gave us two pieces of paper explaining how to apply for the program - scraps of paper, not full-size pages - stapled together.

An IMSS official explained the program to about seventy other people sitting and standing, all of them younger than we were. Maybe two thirds were women, some obviously pregnant, with men beside them. We were the only non-Mexicans. Lupita asked a couple of questions to confirm our basic understanding that we were eligible to apply. She told us the woman said we could enroll after the meeting. I figured it was first-come-first-served, so I left *el auditorio* in search of the application location and someone who could *habla inglés*.

Downstairs I found someone who led me to someone else who led me to an administrator who was willing to meet with us. She confirmed the details, *si*, but explained Sandy and Debbie could not enroll that day because they needed to have their birth certificates translated into *español* by an official translator and certified by *el Notario*. That requirement was not in the application instructions, and it would take a few more days. We left happy with our progress and began looking forward to the third trip.

I had heard good and bad comments about IMSS from Mexicans, including Rosella, who said she received good care during both her pregnancies. Some others complained they couldn't get *agua purificada* to drink while they were in the hospital, and the facilities were not very clean.

On the way back to the car I asked Lupita how she liked the IMSS health care program.

"I don't like it," she said, complaining about the medical attention her older daughter received in an IMSS hospital during a serious illness. Furthermore, she hated the bureaucracy.

IMSS was better than nothing, she agreed, and it was relatively affordable. Based on the fee schedule on one of the scraps of paper, I calculated the annual fees for her family of five totaled about $517 US. For someone my age, it would be about $247 US. It seems like a bargain, and Sandy and Debbie plan to buy into it.

Of course an ounce of prevention is worth a pound of cure, as the old saying goes. Adapting to the Baja lifestyle had already improved my health. Maybe I could prevent, or at least postpone, some future health problems.

When I retired in September of 2007 I was about eighty pounds heavier than when I graduated from high school, and I was chubby even back then. Walking between my office and the D.C. Metro subway system was a daily chore in my last year of work, and I huffed and puffed climbing three flights of stairs in my office building. I struggled to keep my blood pressure lower than 160/90, despite a triple combination of medications for hypertension.

Living in Baja made life less stressful and more enjoyable. I was also able to cut back to one hypertension medication. Eating Mexican restaurant dishes made it hard to lose much weight, but about ten pounds disappeared by late summer of 2008. I started cooking and eating at home as much as possible and dropped another ten pounds by early 2009.

Eventually I went to a health fair at Velmar Hospital in Ensenada. The three-hour event included blood pressure readings and a finger stick for diabetes risk, followed by a twenty-minute overview in the conference room from the head of the hospital. About twenty five of us also sat through two presentations by other doctors—one about health problems associated with aging and one about heart attacks. The medical presentations emphasized prevention and healthy lifestyles including exercise, eating right, taking an aspirin every day, and having a daily glass or two of wine. The wine advice drew cheers from the audience.

A short tour of the hospital revealed state-of-the-art facilities, including an open MRI, emergency rooms, surgical rooms, an intensive care unit, maternity ward, and private patient rooms with very comfortable upholstered futons for family members to stay with patients. The estimated total cost for hospitalization and physician care in the ICU was $1,000 per day, compared with $10,000 or more in the U.S.

The ten-year-old private hospital was almost empty. There were no lines, only a few patients in the patient rooms, no babies in the maternity ward, no patients in the ICU, and no patients in surgery or the ER. Maybe the movie "Field of Dreams" was right - "If you build it, they will come" - but they had not come to Velmar Hospital yet.

During 2009 family and friends talked me into trying to change my food choices, focusing more on locally grown fresh food, much of it organic. Rosemary, who organizes *el organico mercado* twice a month at Poco Cielo in La Misión, insisted that I read *"The Omnivore's Dilemma,"* Michael Pollan's 2006 book about intelligent eating. I started buying her organic produce, *queso*, whole grain *pan,* and other goodies grown or prepared in the nearby *Valle de Guadalupe.*

Organic Market at Poco Cielo

I'm not saying I changed my total diet; fish and shrimp tacos are hard to forgo. However, I developed a strong preference for fettuccine with homemade pasta sauce made from organic sun dried tomatoes, garlic, herbs, and *aceite de oliva.*[24] I began serving guests tasty dishes with wild-caught seafood and true "free-range" chicken or grass-

---

[24] Olive oil

fed beef, without antibiotics. Fortunately, Baja has an abundant local supply of these healthful and tasty foods. Friends and neighbors commented on how much my cooking improved after I switched from spaghetti covered with soup.

In late 2009 I decided to buy an annual $129 membership with Serena Senior Care, a two-year old company offering a range of services to the expatriate community on the Baja Gold Coast. The service is similar to buying an AAA card back in the USA for travel. The membership includes an initial doctor visit to obtain a medical profile, which goes into the Serena database along with personal contact information. If a member needs assistance, just call the hotline number 24/7 and Serena will dispatch medical responders and contact family members back in the USA. That sounds better than calling 066 for *Cruz Roja*. They also provide caretakers as medical needs increase, or assisted living in their own facility. They can also help with non-medical services such as roadside assistance, plumbers and electricians, and pet sitters.

After thirty minutes of completing background information forms I had my little green membership card in my pocket, with its toll free phone number for calls from anywhere in North America. They also gave me an information packet to share with my emergency contact person in Baja and with my next of kin back in the USA. The last step was going for my free initial office visit with a personal care physician from their referral list and getting lab work to complete my medical information profile.

The physician they referred me to has office hours on Tuesdays at the Calafia hotel complex, about six miles south of downtown Rosarito. At my first consultation in the fall of 2009, I discovered I had lost more than twenty-five pounds in my two years of living in Baja. However, my blood pressure was not much lower than before I retired.

Back in Maryland, my previous doctor usually gave me a sample of some new medications to try and said to come back in a couple of weeks. In Baja, *la doctora* wanted several diagnostic tests before prescribing or changing medications. She even suggested a hemoglobin test to benchmark for diabetes risk. That really impressed me because, just before I retired, I had to argue twice with the doctor back in Maryland before he would request the same test.

Paying for lab tests is one minor negative in using Mexican health care providers. I had planned to take the script from my new physician and go to a diagnostics lab in the U.S., using my Blue Cross/Blue Shield insurance. However, Fritz, a new neighbor in Plaza del Mar, said my insurance probably wouldn't cover the tests. He said he knew of cases where insurance companies rejected payment for U.S. lab tests ordered by foreign doctors, and the patients had to pay big bucks to the diagnostic labs. I checked with Debbie, who is a medical billing expert for a company in the USA. She agreed with Fritz. Jo Ann, sales manager for Serena, also agreed.

All of them explained that USA insurance companies would probably insist on having a participating physician in their network request the tests, not a physician in a foreign country. Jo Ann's reasoning was that insurers want USA doctors to reduce diagnostic costs. Maybe that explains why my doctor back in Maryland didn't want to order the hemoglobin test. I asked a couple of follow-up questions.

"You mean they don't want to pay to diagnose a potential problem? What kind of system is that?"

To be certain, I called my insurance company to see if it would pre-approve the diagnostic lab costs. The nice customer service rep said she would need the medical codes for each test and said I could get the codes from my participating physician in the provider network. I said my new doctor wasn't in the provider network, and she said pre-approval required codes from a participating physician. I gave up and went to a lab in Rosarito, where the total out-of-pocket expense for seven specific tests was only $138 US.

The co-pay charges for the tests in the USA might have been that much.

You may have noticed that I refer to my Mexican physician as "she." Having Maria Guadalupe take my medical history and examine me was a little disconcerting at first. That's partly because she's almost thirty years younger than I am and looks a lot like Catherine Zeta-Jones in a doctor role. I was more comfortable by the time we finished the initial consultation before the examination. We even had a good laugh when she asked me the standard male question about erectile dysfunction.

"I don't really know," I chuckled, explaining that I had been separated for a couple of years. "Is there a test for that?"

"Yes," she replied with a quick laugh, "and maybe it's time you found someone to test it again."

Hey, there is no requirement that my physician has to be male, or older, or less attractive, or without a good sense of humor.

Mi doctora wants me to walk at least thirty minutes every day, which I try to do. Still, I need to exercise more and eat less. There are many miles to walk and pounds to lose before I achieve my goal of getting back to my high school weight.

Back in the USA I have a new doctor, who also takes good care of me. I check in with her every six months or so, to update my records and maintain my U.S. insurance coverage. Someday, just in case, I might buy one of the international medical insurance policies that covers private physicians and private hospitals in Mexico.

For now, I feel assured that I can get quality medical care from Maria Guadalupe, at a cost of only $25 US for a sixty-minute office visit.

I Love Baja!

Chapter 21:
The RV Life

Taking Baja roadtrips in a RV motor home appeals to many people, as I noticed on the nineteen-day trip to *Baja California Sur* in February with Sandy and Debbie. We met many RVers parked right on the beaches in spectacular coves along the Sea of Cortez, paying as little as $7 a night for a piece of paradise.

RVs Parked on the Sea of Cortez at El Requéson

A couple of months after the trip Sandy and her former neighbor Bobbie found a used RV sitting in a San Diego neighborhood, and she bought it on the spot. She and Debbie might take it to Colonet and camp out for weeks at a time during the winter. She used to do that out in the California desert in a camper she owned years ago.

I agreed to help Sandy move the RV to Baja after a Saturday yard sale in San Diego at Bobbie's house. During the yard sale, Bobbie reminded Sandy that she needed to have the carburetor cleaned and serviced. Otherwise, the 1984 RV might not make it back to Baja, especially going up the big hill out of Tijuana heading south to Rosarito. Sandy was enjoying the yard sale, so she gave me a handful of $20 bills to take the RV to a carburetor repair shop in Chula Vista about twenty minutes south toward the border. I had never driven an RV, but how hard could it be?

"It drives like a car," Bobbie assured me, although it was twenty-four-feet long and weighed at least twice as much. The only way to see behind it was to use the oversize rear view mirrors sticking out from the sides of the cab. She told me to be back before 4 p.m., because she was having a "surprise" cookout for Sandy's birthday party.

On the way back, after I got off the I-5 near Balboa Park, the RV died going up a hill alongside a golf course. It coughed and sputtered and just quit. It had all the signs of being out of gas. I steered it into the bike lane next to the golf course fence and called AAA to say I needed help. The customer service woman wanted to know my location, so I hollered through the fence at a foursome ready to tee off and asked them where I was. Wherever she was, the AAA lady had trouble understanding how the RV ran out of gas next to the twelfth tee at a golf course. But I talked her through it, and about thirty minutes later a pickup truck with big AAA letters on it delivered free gas. It was a beautiful sight.

The RV dual gas tanks had new locking caps, but none of the keys on the key ring would work, not even the ones that said GAS in big letters. I called Bobbie and told her to start the party without me. She explained the situation to Sandy, who said to have the AAA guy break off one of the locked caps. He didn't want to, even after I assured him that the owner said it was okay. But after I offered him a $20 bill, he grabbed a hammer and a screwdriver, popped the gas cap, and poured in enough gas to get me to a service station.

The RV started, but it died again after ten seconds. The AAA guy tried it too, with the same results. It wouldn't start at all after two or three more times. Therefore, he agreed to call for a tow truck. It was a beautiful sight too, coming up the hill to rescue me.

It was one of those tow trucks with a long bed that slides back and tilts down, and then uses a winch with cables to pull a disabled vehicle up the incline. When the winch started pulling the RV up the inclined bed, the tow truck driver and I discovered that the RV was not out of gas. In fact the tank with the missing gas cap was full, and gas started sloshing out of the tank where the locked gas cap used to be. In a matter of seconds we were causing an environmental incident with gasoline spreading across the asphalt and trickling down the hill.

The simplest option seemed to be to keep loading the RV onto the tow truck and get out of there. I walked down the hill and waved traffic around the disaster area while the tow truck driver finished loading the RV. We pulled away, I gave him the name of the auto repair place Sandy wanted to use, and he eased along the streets to keep from sloshing out more gasoline while we were moving.

It was after 5 p.m. by then and the repair place was closed, gates shut with chains and big padlocks. The only available place to park the RV was on the street in front of the locked gates with its rear end pointed down the hill. However, the RV would not roll off the inclined bed easily, because its back bumper hung over the rear axle too far. The tow truck driver started jockeying the inclined bed back and forth, sloshing more gasoline out of the tank and creating another mini-environmental spill.

I had him stop so we could get something to plug the gas tank fill pipe. He borrowed a gas cap from an old van parked on the street, a brilliant bit of ingenuity. But it wouldn't fit the RV. The only thing I could find was a big wad of paper towels from the AM-PM mini-mart at a gas station on the corner—not very ingenious. It didn't work either.

While he finished unloading the RV, I stood across the street, hoping nobody tossed a lighted cigarette from a passing car. A walker stopped to watch for a moment, unaware of my involvement with the RV. Great; a witness—the only thing missing now was a police cruiser with flashing lights. About that time, Sandy's ex-husband Kevin arrived to fetch me and we watched together as the scene unfolded. I hoped the RV wouldn't break loose and roll backwards down the hill and into the intersection forty yards away.

The tow truck driver knew his stuff, and the cables held. Soon, all four tires of the RV were on the pavement—sitting in gasoline—but on the pavement. The driver had to lie on his back in the gasoline and wriggle underneath the RV to unhook the cables. Fortunately, nobody drove by with a lighted cigarette.

All I had to do was get the RV out of the street and over to the curb, in front of the locked gates to the repair shop. Of course, it wouldn't start. I would have to muscle it using dead power steering and power brakes, let it roll backwards down the hill, steer it around two parked vehicles, and parallel park it. I let it roll, looking into the rear view mirrors, and standing on the brake pedal with both feet. Somehow, it managed to snuggle up to the curb close to where I was aiming. Now that was truly a beautiful sight. Even the tow truck driver was impressed.

I felt sorry for the driver, grime on his gloves and shirtsleeves, gasoline on the back of his shirt and pants, and I gave him two of those $20 bills. He liked them as much as the first guy. I should have given him more of them, but I wanted to save one or two to give back to Sandy.

The birthday party for Sandy was pretty much over by the time we arrived back at Bobbie's place. I missed Sandy's daughter bringing the birthday cake, everybody singing "Happy Birthday," and Sandy blowing out the candle. Nevertheless, there was plenty of food left, and Debbie had waited to give me a ride back to Baja.

Headed back to Baja after the party, I started laughing about all the things that happened. What really made me laugh was thinking about how much worse the situation would have been if the RV had died going up the big hill in Tijuana.

The original concept for the RV was something Sandy and Debbie thought of during the February roadtrip to southern Baja. I was skeptical, because I recalled when I owned an old thirty-seven-foot wooden motor yacht back on the Chesapeake Bay and how it kept costing more and more. To me, an RV sounded much like a boat with wheels. I declined Sandy's offer to let me buy into ownership of the RV, but Debbie bought a half interest. She helped Sandy figure out how to insure it in Mexico and how to buy roadside assistance in Baja from the Good Sam Club. That seemed absolutely critical for a twenty-five-year-old vehicle, especially after it stalled that day by the golf course.

After they spent a couple of months and several hundred dollars to get the RV running in San Diego, it was ready for the trip to Baja. All of us went together to get it at the repair shop and drive it back to Sandy's place. Debbie followed us back to Baja, just in case we broke down or something else went wrong. I explained that Sandy had to ride in the RV because the registered owner must be with a vehicle when it crosses the border. Mexican authorities want to see all the paperwork, including proof of ownership and Mexican insurance. At least, that's what it says in my little book about the Mexican legal system. At a minimum, border *policía* were likely to stop us and search the RV.

Sure enough, the book was right. *La policía* waved us over, asked for the papers, and opened the rear door to look inside. It wasn't a thorough search, just a quick look, and we were on our way again in a few minutes. I guess we looked safe enough—two senior citizens, heading into Baja, driving an old RV. It probably happens often.

The 1984 RV

We turned right to take the toll road bypassing Tijuana, although it meant driving up that big hill I laughed about earlier. It runs alongside the border fence, with almost no room to pull over onto the shoulder if you have vehicle trouble. The hill is a couple of miles long, and the last part is steeper than the rest. Sometimes, my ears pop just before the crest of the hill.

The RV climbed the first part of the hill easily enough. On the last part a slow moving car, maybe older than the RV, was poking along ahead of us in our lane. That was potential trouble, because I wasn't sure how much power the RV would have going uphill at a very low speed. So, I changed lanes, pushed the gas pedal to the metal, and lumbered into the passing lane.

How slow was the other vehicle? I'm not sure, but you know a car is really slow when a twenty-five-year-old RV passes it on the Tijuana hill. It was a little like a turtle passing a snail. Debbie said later she couldn't believe I tried it, but the RV made it fine.

The guard at the gate to our community gave Sandy a funny look when we arrived, because the HOA rules prohibit RVs, boats, etc. Sandy can be a charmer, however, and he let us through the gate. We eased down the hill and parked in front of her oceanfront condo. I noticed that the brakes seemed a little soft, but I was able to get it into a parking spot with the rear end sticking out into the street only a little.

It was hard to overlook a RV parked in a residential space, and right away neighbors stopped by to look. Some wanted to check out the interior. Apparently many folks fantasize about RV roadtrips. It was a couple of days before the HOA rules police became involved and informed Sandy and Debbie the RV had to go.

They avoided a confrontation by arranging to take it to a mechanic to check the brakes. The mechanic discovered the brakes were worn out; we were lucky we didn't use them very much on the trip from San Diego into Baja. After the mechanic fixed the brakes, Debbie drove the RV back to the community and parked it up the hill in a driveway in front of some half-finished houses—just for a day or two—until they could find a home for it outside the community.

Next day a groundskeeper appeared at Debbie's house and told her she had to move it, and she said okay. When she didn't comply right away, the HOA vice president showed up at her door with the uniformed police security guard armed with his WWII military surplus carbine. That provoked a shouting match that upset almost everybody, at least the ones who heard about it. Summoning an armed guard seemed unnecessary, especially to deal with two grandmothers who simply wanted a used RV for roadtrips now and then. *El seguridado* apologized to her, and she knew it wasn't his doing.

Sandy and Debbie took the RV to the community next door, which had a boat or two and a car that may not be in running order, and where Georgiann's son John lived. They parked it out of the way near his house in a corner of the community. All was well for a week or so. Then somebody from the HOA over there figured out that the RV didn't belong to John, and they had to move it again.

Debbie and I drove around one afternoon looking for places to move it—someplace that didn't charge much of anything and where it would be safe. Gated campgrounds and even a friend of a friend in a rural area wanted more than she was willing to pay. With time running out the best solution was to park it inside the fenced yard of Sandy's housekeeper's son Francesco Junior, down in the valley at La Misión about four miles away.

Sandy and Debbie took it for their first roadtrip, a shakedown cruise of maybe forty miles, to a campground just south of Ensenada that had hookups so they could check out all the RV systems. They reported that the RV made the trip fine. However, they learned that some things did not work well.

The AC didn't blow cold air and that would be a problem on trips to warmer places. The water system worked fine but the toilet didn't flush. The electric system provided electricity but the refrigerator didn't get cold. The stereo didn't play the way it did when the previous owner demonstrated it to Sandy on the day she bought the RV for $2,000 in a spur-of-the-moment decision. And it had no Internet connection.

But those were little things. With a little TLC, surely the RV would be just fine for longer roadtrips later. I wasn't so sure. After all, they had not mentioned what to do about their five dogs and five cats they discussed on our roadtrip back in February. And I noticed they didn't take any animals with them on the overnight trip.

A couple of weeks later Debbie found a new RV toilet and propane refrigerator on the Internet and arranged the purchase by phone. The place was a RV sales and service center in San Diego, and the guy on the phone offered to obtain the equipment offsite so the cost would be less than the normal retail price. Sandy took her SUV to get the RV equipment and I hitched a ride to the USA with her because I wanted to pick up some discount wine. For medicinal purposes, as recommended by the doctors at Velmar Hospital.

Of course, when you're buying expensive RV equipment under-the-counter you can't just walk into the store and pay for it at the sales counter. Sandy went in and found the guy who was Debbie's contact. She came out a few minutes later, fussing and fuming.

"The guy changed the price, and he's ripping us off," she said. She called Debbie in Baja. Debbie called the guy's cell phone and he confirmed the original agreed upon price. He explained he couldn't discuss it at the counter. Then she called Sandy, who handed the phone to me because she couldn't hear clearly.

"Maybe she's having trouble with her hearing aids," Debbie told me. "Or maybe she didn't understand what he said. Just do the deal."

Also, when you buy something that way, you have to pay cash. So Sandy went to a bank and withdrew $2,000—$1,500 for the equipment and enough for the Mexican customs tax. She called the contact and he told her to meet him in a nearby shopping center in about 30 minutes. She couldn't understand the name of the shopping center so she handed me the phone. I told her I hoped nobody was monitoring the cell phone calls because it sounded like people arranging a drug deal.

I also asked how she could trust this total stranger not to send an accomplice who would stick a gun in her face and take the money. Her solution was to park in front of the Mega-Spin laundromat where people were sitting around waiting for their laundry to finish. She divided the cash and asked me to hold some of it—now if the cops showed up, there was evidence in my pocket that I was a buyer too.

Almost right on time, a guy in a little car with dark tinted windows drove up alongside and told her to follow him to get the goods. She was sure it was the same guy she talked to in the first store earlier in the morning. We drove behind him for a couple of miles to another store that sold RV supplies. After we squeezed into a parking space on the street, he walked back to her window and asked for the money.

"How can I be sure you won't just take the cash and drive away?" she asked him. He handed her his car keys as a sign of good faith. However, Sandy isn't anybody's fool.

"How do I know that's your car?" she asked. "Maybe it's stolen." I began to think she had done this kind of thing before. "Give me your driver's license," she demanded.

He seemed surprised but he gave her his license. We gave him all the money and he walked into the nearby store. He came back out in a few minutes with some paperwork and asked us to follow him to pick up the goods at a warehouse a few blocks away. He asked her to return his license to drive over there. Sandy said he would get it back when she got the stuff.

The contact handled the transaction with the people at the warehouse and they loaded the unopened cartons into the back of Sandy's SUV. However, she wanted to make certain the equipment was what she was buying. She made them open the cartons. It was a little like scenes in the movies where the buyers ask to see the goods before shaking hands and driving away. I just sat in the passenger seat hoping for the best. Sandy got back behind the wheel, fastened her seat belt, and started laughing. She recognized the place from years ago when she and her ex-husband bought parts for their old camper.

"You know what?" she asked me. "We could have done the whole deal ourselves without paying the middleman."

After getting my wine and buying some supplies, we sat in the rush hour traffic jam on the 805 highway headed into Mexico just before dark. I was driving and we were munching Costco sushi when I reminded her that we needed to declare the RV equipment to Mexican customs officials. A case of wine was not a problem because each of us could bring in a few bottles without paying a duty. However, $1,500 worth of new RV equipment still in the cartons was another matter.

"Forget it," she said. "I don't feel like paying customs on the RV stuff. Maybe they won't stop us."

I moved left into in the middle lanes, away from the *Declaraciõn* lanes at the right for voluntarily declaring we were importing something of value. We bumped over the speed bumps, and the surveillance cameras apparently thought we looked innocent enough. The Mexican border agent in our lane kept waving us forward and the light blinked green.

"I CANNOT believe they didn't stop us," Sandy gushed as we crossed the borderline and headed for the road to bypass Tijuana. "Can you believe it? WOW!"

She was looking forward to the first real Baja roadtrip with the RV, just as soon as she found somebody to install the new equipment and repair the AC. Maybe to San Felipé for the annual shrimp festival or maybe the observatory in a national park 9,000 feet up in the Baja mountains.

Sandy learned from a guy who cleaned her upholstery one day that he knew somebody who could install the RV equipment. She and Debbie took it to the cleaner's home and he arranged the repairs there. The repairman didn't have time to fix the generator because Sandy was eager to take a trip. With a new fridge and toilet, she and Debbie took off for their first RV weekend trip, to the shrimp festival. I couldn't go with them because I had already committed to another of those joint Baja birthday parties. Independently, both of them told me bits and pieces of what happened.

First, they didn't leave until about 2 p.m. That made it almost impossible to get over the mountains between

Ensenada and San Felipé before dark. Then they became lost in Ensenada trying to find the turn for Route 3 heading for the mountains. So they stopped overnight near a roadside motel/cafe in the *Ojos Negro* agricultural valley about thirty-six miles past Ensenada toward the mountains. That was the advantage of RV travel, they said—you could just stop anywhere. There were no electrical hookups and it was a three-blanket night.

They weren't impressed with the shrimp festival the next afternoon so they headed south looking for Puertecitos, a quaint little village that some describe as the proverbial nowhere. No RV hookups, no electricity, not much of anything. Sal and Maria, who live in the San Felipé area, tried to call them several times and invite them to stay at their place. Their cell phones couldn't receive a signal.

Throughout the trip, they kept worrying that they were going to run out of gas because the fuel gauge didn't work. That could have been a real problem according to the Internet,[25] which states: "The gasoline situation in Puertecitos is iffy. Sometimes they have it, sometimes they don't."

They flipped the switch to change to the backup tank and discovered that the gas flow wouldn't work right unless they were on level ground. That's probably what happened to me on the hill at Balboa Park. They stopped frequently to top off the main tank, which is how they learned the old RV was a gas hog. However, they made it back home safely. Debbie said later the RV got less than five mpg. Maybe.

"It might be better to just park it somewhere down south and use it as a getaway place," she told me ruefully. Driving it cost too much.

I was looking forward to the next RV trip, or at least hearing about it.

Finding somebody to work on vehicles in Baja is easy—all you have to do is say you need something, and half a dozen

---

[25] http://www.bajaexpo.com/cities/puertec.htm

people will say they know somebody who knows somebody. That's how they found people to work on the RV, and how I fixed most things on my Caravan and the Suburban. Many times, the vehicle fixers also have other talents, like *el mecánico* Roberto, who fixed my headlight and bumper, but who actually worked for his father's auto audio shop. Some offer to import vehicles, install car alarms, or handle vehicle registration and insurance.

I needed the Suburban AC to blow cold air for a roadtrip to Southern Baja, so friends referred me to a place that had used refrigerators lined up on the side of the road. They had to replace the compressor with one they found in a junkyard. The automatic thermostat didn't work, so they got an electrician friend to install a manual on-off toggle switch on the dash. The whole repair, including parts and labor and new Freon, was only $90 US.

Dave and Christy, friends from Las Vegas who own a place in Baja next to Debbie, have a great story about "Mexi-rigging." When they were younger, they took Baja weekend getaways to a trailer Dave's family owned in a KOA campground, with a great ocean view. At one time, Christy owned a new 1978 Thunderbird, which had ignition problems that baffled trained Ford mechanics back in the states. Sure enough, on one trip to Baja, the T-bird died in the campground.

Dave hitchhiked into Rosarito Beach and found a little garage that was open on Sunday. He told the guy it was a Ford, and the guy's face lit up in a big smile because Mexicans have a lot of experience working on old Ford vehicles. They hitched a ride together back to the campground in the bed of a pickup. The guy looked under the T-bird hood and came up with the obvious solution—just hot-wire the ignition. Luckily, there was a piece of insulated wire in the back of the pickup.

"The guy just stripped the insulation off the ends with his teeth, hooked up the wire, and the T-bird roared to life," says Dave.

"I kept the wire and used it many more times," says Christy.

My favorite example of the multi-talented automotive workforce in Baja is that tiny roadside *llantera* in La Misión, the one where Sandy and Debbie fantasized about the well-muscled *hombre*. It also has a sign advertising *"reparacion de transmision automaticas."*[26] The makeshift building has only three sides and is open to the hillside at the back. The roof is blue polytarp, which is in tatters from the weather. I see vehicles there now and then, parked on the side of the highway, sitting on a jack, while somebody works on a tire. I never see anybody working on transmissions, and I'm always skeptical about their capabilities.

Tire Shop and Transmission Repairs in La Misión

On the other hand, if a guy from a little garage can solve a T-bird ignition problem with a piece of wire and his teeth, maybe the little *llantera* can handle transmission repairs.

---

[26] Automatic transmission repair

Chapter 22:
Fiddler On The Beach

Good musicians hanging out in Baja between concert tours and recording sessions are hidden treasures. People find out about their laid-back music sessions by word of mouth or email alerts.

Some friends in Baja invited me to hear fiddler Alex DePue, who was getting ready for the annual Grand Master Fiddler Championship in Nashville. He was playing for tips at a little place right on the Pacific Ocean at the K-58 campground, about thirty-six miles south of the border, on the city limits between Rosarito and Ensenada.

The thatched-roof open-air palapa had a small bar in the left rear corner, and tables and chairs for about seventy people in the main part. In the right rear corner, a stage with two spotlights and a one-microphone sound system sat waiting between sets. An unpretentious guy, in his late thirties, walked over and welcomed us.

"Thanks for coming," he said. "I'm Alex."

He smiled broadly and stuck out his hand with a strong handshake. He stepped onto the one-step-high small stage, settled onto a hard swivel chair, and shouted hello to three other new arrivals. A tiny table sat in front of the stage, holding a metal pot with a sign saying "Tips" surrounded by his business cards and maybe a dozen copies of two CDs. He said they would make great Christmas stocking stuffers and joked that they were only "$20 apiece, or two for $50."

He took a box of cigarettes from his shirt pocket and tossed it into his open fiddle case on the floor. He pulled the electric fiddle close to his chest, hugged it with his neck, and drew the bow across the strings.

The fiddle began singing and dancing a Cajun tune, with Alex keeping time by stomping his right foot on the plywood stage. The fiddle moaned long and low, like a locomotive whistle, on the opening notes of *Orange Blossom Special*, a tune many consider the American national anthem for fiddle players. He reached out with his bow and tapped it twice on the metal pot to make a sound like a locomotive bell. Then the fiddle picked up speed and exploded into the breakneck tempo of the 1938 bluegrass classic.

He treated the handful of people to a practice set for the fiddle championship, three tunes in four minutes. The fiddle twanged to the bluegrass classic *Sally Goodin*, swung into waltz tempo for *The Yellow Rose of Texas*, and finished in a frenzy with *Wild Fiddler's Rag*.

Another night, he started a game of "Name That Tune," demonstrating his versatility on half a dozen pieces from Lionel Ritchie, the Eagles, and others. People at the tables shouted out names of songs they recognized, and softly sang the words they knew.

He paused to encourage requests. "Just write what you want to hear on a $10 bill and give it to me," Alex joked. The fiddle launched into *Smoke On The Water,* with everybody clapping time. Somebody asked for *The Devil Went Down to Georgia*, a country classic.

"That's a $50-dollar request," he teased, but he played it anyway. He sang the lyrics too, and the place went crazy.

His cheek-length hair fell across his face, whipping from side to side as he swayed, and he stomped that right foot on the stage, sweat soaking through his shirt. He finished the evening with a wave of his fiddle bow, and the crowd of twenty eight cheered enthusiastically. Some guests dropped money into the tip bucket and began drifting out, but others stayed to visit for a minute or two. My front row seat cost just $2.50 for a cup of *café Mexicano*, plus tips for the metal pot.

Listening to two of his Baja sessions gave me new appreciation for violin virtuosity, and I could hear why Alex is one of the best in the world. His fantastic fiddling included bluegrass, rock, and Bach. He performed one classical music piece written for four violins. Two friends from Los Angeles saw him another night and came away impressed, wanting to know more about him.

Alex began studying classical violin when he was five, won his first major competition when he was just ten years old, performed at Carnegie Hall at age sixteen, and has performed in fiddle championships across the USA. In 2007, he won the California State Fiddle Championship. He won fourth place in the Grand Master Fiddle Championship in 2005, and won eighth place in 2008. Back in 2007, he toured North America, South America, and Europe with legendary rock guitarist Steve Vai. In Mexico he usually tours with Miguel de Hoyos, a great Mexican classical guitarist also from Baja. Videos from some of their performances are on the Internet.[27]

In Baja, Alex and Miguel hang out in the La Misión area, but also play gigs in southern Baja. Usually the places they play have a $10 cover charge, which their local booking agent Nuria tries to collect from all patrons while also hawking CDs from the duo. Sometimes they practice and play just for tips.

By himself, Miguel is a guitar virtuoso with a good voice and a 500-song repertoire in Spanish and Italian and English that includes crowd pleasers such as *Stairway to Heaven*, *Hotel California* and *Sweet Caroline*. Herb and

---

[27] http://www.myspace.com/alexdepue

Marina and Jacki and Jack and Barb and I went to hear him one night at the Half Way House, along with fourteen other paying customers. He delighted the dinner crowd by playing three long sets over four hours, mostly Spanish songs, taking requests from everybody. His fingers flew over the strings in flamenco rhythms as we clapped hands to keep time; his version of *Spanish Eyes* caused one woman to weep. Even Chef Johnny joined in, coming out of the kitchen in his chef's tunic after dinner and singing a heartfelt rendition of the Italian classic *O Solo Mio* while Miguel accompanied him.

Live music is a big part of life in Baja, all around the peninsula. Trios and quartets and quintets of mariachi musicians stroll city sidewalks carrying guitars and accordions, lugging bass fiddles and holding brass trumpets sometimes, wearing pressed pants and starched shirts. They take turns going into restaurants up and down the main boulevards in Ensenada and Rosarito on weekends, walking between the tables of diners, soliciting requests and tips. In larger restaurants along the Gold Coast, Mexican bands like Wandana set up drums and keyboards and plug in electric guitars on weekends, alternating sets sometimes with an eight-piece mariachi band wearing embroidered jackets and cowboy hats.

Musicians less well known than Alex and Miguel make regular rounds of restaurants along Route 1, playing for tips here one night and there another. Some are Mexicans, some are gringos; some are good, some aren't. Some of the best are Ross with his guitar and rock and country songs, Paco with his Spanish guitar, Maryam with her Whitney Houston vocal range, and Sue with her mellow vocals.

No matter who else is playing, nothing beats the experience of listening to Alex and Miguel. They fill the room with spectacular sounds even when the room and the tip jar are almost empty. One night at Poco Cielo, some of us went to hear the dynamic duo perform again. My friends Ruben and Frances were there from California, and Rowan from Ensenada and two of her friends, and Jack. Plus eight other customers, two of whom said they recently moved to Baja from Nashville.

Miguel began strumming a tango rhythm and a young couple sitting at the bar got up and began dancing. They clutched and kicked, swirled and swayed, and stirred the souls in all of us. We rewarded them with applause, and they rewarded us with a second dance. We stood to cheer, appreciating the music and their dance of lovers.

Two very talented dancers. Alex and Miguel. Ten dollars for a seat fifteen feet in front of them. One night in La Misión.

It doesn't get much better than that.

I Love Baja!

Chapter 23:

Rosella

I'm not sure how well I could function in Baja without Rosella's help. She is very reliable in everything I ask her to do and almost indispensable.

At first, she was just my immigration agent. In addition to immigration tasks, she completed the Mexican Power of Attorney for my middle son, translated it, arranged the official certification, and filed it with a *Notario*. She helped me get my Mexican driver's license and Baja license plates for my van. When I couldn't get GEICO or State Farm or AAA to insure my Mexican van in the USA, she arranged insurance through a Mexican company. She helped me prepare and file my Certification of Ratification instructing Mexican authorities how to handle my death, if I die in Mexico. Soon she began helping me with many aspects of an expat life in Mexico and became my primary provider-of-insights into Mexican life.

I was talking one day with Sandy, Debbie, and Georgiann about how much I rely on Rosella. Georgiann said it sounded like I was sweet on her. However, I don't think of her romantically and she certainly would never think of me that way. We have become trusted friends—*amigos de confianza*—although she always calls me "Mr. Miller." We can talk about almost anything. It's much like my relationship with Deshiree, my close friend and former co-worker back in Maryland, the same age as Rosella.

Rosella

One time Rosella told me about a client who invited her and her kids to spend the weekend at his oceanfront home a few weeks after his terminally ill wife died. She took Alejandra and her daughter from Ensenada for company, just to be proper. He invited her to come back again, and offered to let her borrow his new car now and then.

Afterward, she wanted to know from me what the client meant when he told her he wanted to have some "one-on-one time" with her, maybe on a trip to Las Vegas or on a shopping trip to New York City. I explained what I thought he had in mind. She grimaced.

"*El es un hombre viejo,*"[28] she said, explaining he was sixty. I laughed, because I was sixty five.

---

[28] He is an old man.

I Love Baja!

Over two years, I met three *hombres* who obviously liked her a lot. She wanted my opinion of them, so maybe she was thinking about remarriage someday. However, she still has the mental scars from her first husband and her first priority is raising her children. Besides, she laughs, she hasn't met anyone yet who can afford the lifestyle she wants.

Raising *dos niños* without much money has to be hard for her. She makes some extra money by cutting and styling hair at night and on weekends, plus what I pay her for tasks. Nevertheless, she doesn't complain, at least to me. Her *madre* gives her a break on the rent for her house across the back street, and I'm pretty sure she also takes up the slack with education and presents for the *nietos*, like the birthday party for José Carlos.

Rosella was unable to get alimony from her ex-husband. The court ordered just 500 pesos a week for combined child support. Her longer-term concern is how to pay for the *quinceañera* Paola Nicole wants, the traditional Spanish celebration for a 15th birthday. Rosella says they will find a way somehow. They already reserved a location more than a year ahead.

Before I began buying my medicine in Baja, I drove to San Diego to refill my prescriptions using my USA insurance plan. Just before a trip in mid November 2008, I asked Rosella and her mother if they wanted me to get anything for them. Rosella said she needed a favor. She wanted to take her kids shopping in San Diego, using her Christmas bonus from her job at her mother's office. She asked if I could take all of them with me on Saturday. I said okay. By the way, she said with a little laugh, she was entitled to a bonus from me now that she was doing some additional work for me. She and her mother explained the Mexican custom is to give all workers a Christmas bonus. I figured it wouldn't hurt me, and Rosella does a lot of good things for me.

A couple of days before the trip, she said a friend in San Diego offered to take her and the kids to the San Diego

Zoo on Sunday. Paola Nicole and José Carlos were excited because they had never been to a zoo. That meant we would have to stay over Saturday night to accommodate both shopping and the zoo. *No hay problema.* I called a motel on the San Diego harbor, where I had stayed before catching early morning flights back to Maryland, and booked a family room with a king bed and a pullout sofa bed. After all, we were almost *familia*, like *un tio* and his relatives. Rosella and *los niños* would share the bed while I slept on the sofa bed.

The subtlety of the verb "take" is sometimes lost in translation, even in English, even in the USA. I figured her friend's offer might not include paying for zoo tickets at $34 each. We stopped at an ATM just across the border to buy dollars and I got some cash for Rosella's bonus and three zoo tickets. I handed it over to her and said she could spend it however she wanted. We shopped at Plaza de las Americas, a huge mall of name brand outlet stores, until José Carlos and I dropped out and took naps in the van. Rosella and Paola Nicole never tired and day turned into night.

The friend arrived at the motel the next morning to take them to the zoo for the day. I checked out of the motel, took the van, and headed to my pharmacy to have my prescriptions refilled. "Quantum of Solace" was showing at the twenty-four-screen movie theater, and I decided to see my first movie in several months. Afterward, we checked in by phone and met for *la cena* at a little neighborhood Mexican cafe near the border.

I was right about the zoo tickets.

Also, I discovered later in my little book about Mexican laws that fulltime employees are entitled to fifteen days of pay—not just two weeks. The bonus is called *Aguinaldo*[29] and is welcome holiday income. Usually, according to the book, employers pay a bonus equal to a month's salary. Good thing for me that Rosella is an independent contractor and not a fulltime employee.

---

[29] Survival Guide to the Mexican Legal System; Strickland, B.K.; p. 51

During 2009, Rosella became more active in the community of immigration professionals in Rosarito and began handling more of the management of her mother's immigration business. In October, the Rosarito *Asociacion de Profesionales en Tramites Migratorios* (APTM) rewarded her efforts by naming her the new president for a two-year term. She was very excited, and invited me to attend the ceremony when the Mayor installed her and the other officers. I was excited for her too, and proud to sit at her table reserved for family and honored guests.

A couple of weeks later, to honor her achievement, I hosted a little wine and cheese open house at the oceanfront condo I was renting from Sandy in Plaza del Mar. I also asked her to bring Paola Nicole and José Carlos, and Triny from her office, and to invite some of her other friends and family. She invited her sister Aurora and her husband Rafael and kids; her friend Alejandra and Alejandra's mother; and Alejandra's daughter and a daughter's friend.

Several of my friends and neighbors dropped by to meet Rosella and were very impressed. It was a great afternoon of about twenty five *Americanos* and Mexicans spending time together. Rosella and her family and friends stayed after the open house and we cooked Mexican food and grilled hamburgers for the *seis niños*.

After the rest of the guests left, Rosella and Alejandra took a tour of my spacious three-bedroom condo. They were especially impressed with the large Jacuzzi bathtub in the master bathroom. I told them Sandy said her granddaughter liked all the bubbles the Jacuzzi made with bubble bath in her condo upstairs. I invited them to come back some weekend and let the kids try the Jacuzzi. They giggled at the idea of making *burbujas,* the Spanish word for bubbles.

They said okay; however, I suspected they wouldn't come back. Mexicans are too polite to say no to invitations. Sure enough, they couldn't coordinate their schedules and never made it back.

Despite more responsibilities in 2009 at her mother's business, Rosella's financial future is still uncertain. She wants to look for a building lot she can buy with monthly payments, hoping to invest for the future. That requires more monthly income.

In December of 2009, she went back to court in Ensenada to demand that her ex-husband contribute more financially to raising their two children. He agreed to give her an additional 100 pesos per week—an increase of about $8 US at that time.

No siempre puedes tener lo que quieres.

Chapter 24:

Bad People

Living in Baja puts USA expatriates on the defensive because we constantly have to reassure family and friends back home we are safe.

Most of us are secure in the knowledge that violent crime in Baja almost never touches ordinary citizens, tourists, and expats. All the crime statistics from reliable sources in the USA and Mexico show that. Reliable reports throughout the expat community confirm it. Of course, we're aware of sensational news reports about unknown victims of gruesome crimes between rival drug cartels. Usually I brush the news aside, much as people back in the USA do with unwelcome news about murder and high crime rates in other parts of their cities.

That was before somebody tried to kill the daughter of someone I know. The unnerving ordeal grabbed all of us who learned about it, shook us as never before, and altered our perceptions about safety in Baja.

Initial rumors and reports in the expat community said a gang of kidnappers grabbed Cha Cha's seven-month-pregnant daughter and the daughter's boyfriend. People said Cha Cha paid what she could; apparently, the kidnappers wanted more. Police closed in on the gang. Before trying to get away, they cut the daughter's throat. She survived by pretending to be dead. Medics with the police saved her life and police caught most of the gang. The boyfriend was dead.

Two weeks after the incident, Spanish language TV and newspapers reported the man who confessed to the murder told police the boyfriend owed money for a drug debt. Some of the five gang members were USA citizens and lived north of the border. The eighteen-year-old Mexican-American daughter and her twenty-five-year-old Mexican boyfriend knew some of them. The kidnappers didn't wear masks and they didn't blindfold the two victims. Maybe the victims drove voluntarily to the Tijuana apartment where the murder occurred the first day of the ordeal. We may never know everything about the crime.

"You don't need to worry, Mr. Miller," Rosella said after reading the story to me. "You don't know any bad people."

Despite this incident, Baja isn't as dangerous as many places in the U.S. I usually try to reassure people by referring them to the website address for FBI crime statistics.[30] It shows higher murder rates in some surprising cities across the USA, including Baltimore where my youngest son and his wife live.

The 2008 FBI crime statistics identify these USA cities and their murder rates per 100,000:

1.	Camden, NJ	71.05
2.	New Orleans, LA	63.70
3.	St. Louis, MO	46.91
4.	Youngstown, OH	39.79
5.	Saginaw, MI	38.18
6.	Baltimore, MD	36.88
7.	Wilmington, DE	35.17
8.	Washington, DC	31.53
9.	Compton, CA	29.79
10.	Baton Rouge, LA	29.53

---

[30] http://www.fbi.gov/ucr/cius2008/data/table_06.html

Baja has lower murder rates than any of those locations, even counting sensationalized gruesome deaths involving drug cartel violence in Tijuana. For perspective, the estimated population of Tijuana in 2009 was 3.5 million, bigger than Chicago and not that far behind Los Angeles. In 2009, it had 844 murders,[31] about twenty four per 100,000 residents. Rosarito, with an estimated population of about 100,000, had twenty seven murders in 2009. At least ten USA cities—including Washington, DC—had murder rates higher than those.

Other times, I send people hyperlinks to national magazine articles[32] about the most dangerous cities in the USA. Some of the articles include violent crime statistics showing many USA tourist destinations, including Orlando and Las Vegas, have higher violent crime rates than the Baja Gold Coast. I remind them that when people go to Disneyworld or the Vegas strip, usually they are smart enough to avoid dangerous neighborhoods. The same is true in Baja.

Some of the research about crime in Baja comes from the *Centro de Investigación y Docencia Económicas,*[33] a non-profit research entity founded in 1974 as part of the National Council of Science and Technology in Mexico. Its report for 2008 states that the entire state of Baja California had 20.5 homicides per 100,000 population, based on information gathered from the Federal National Security System.

For more perspective, I refer people to a U.S. State Department website[34] that tracks deaths of all U.S. citizens outside the United States. For 2008 and 2009, it reports sixty one deaths of U.S. citizens on the northern Baja coast, all but fourteen of them in Tijuana. The nine deaths in Ensenada

---

[31] http://www.signonsandiego.com/news/2010/jan/24/new-face-border-violence/
[32] http://os.cqpress.com/citycrime/2009/CityCrime2009_Rank_Rev.pdf
[33] http://www.cide.edu/presentation.htm
[34] http://travel.state.gov/law/family_issues/death/deathReport.php?

include four homicides, three auto accidents, one "other accident," and one suicide. The five deaths in Rosarito include two auto accidents, one homicide, one suicide, and one "other accident."

Still, people believe what they want to believe. Someone sent me a highly opinionated article warning readers that drug cartels in Mexico would gun down tourists, behead them, or hang their bodies from highway overpasses. It was a very distorted view without basis in fact. It was also full of untruths and opinions similar to dogma spread by anti-Mexican immigration disciples of right-wing commentators.

I try to push back against such irresponsible attacks, sometimes referring people to a reputable database at *The Houston Chronicle* newspaper that tracks murders of U.S. citizens in Mexico. In all of 2008, according to the database, [35] the only two U.S. citizens murdered in Rosarito or Ensenada were involved with people transporting drugs.

Per capita murder rates in many Caribbean and Latin American countries were higher in 2009 than in Mexico. About.com, a respected website, states four countries in the Caribbean and Latin America have the highest murder rates in the world for each 100,000 residents, right after Iraq:[36]

Venezuela	65.0
El Salvador	55.3
Honduras	49.9
Jamaica	49.0

Some people tell me I'm too defensive. Others say I sound like a PR agent for Baja. Certainly, the Baja Gold Coast has its share of crimes, such as home burglaries and auto theft. Often these crimes involve so-called "targets of opportunity," much like burglarizing homes back in the Maryland suburbs while homeowners are at work or on vacation.

Sometimes people tell me they understand all this.

---

[35] http://www.chron.com/databases/mexicomurders.html
[36] http://gocaribbean.about.com/od/healthandsafety/a/CaribMurder.htm

They think Baja is unsafe for other reasons—"street crime," as an example. Baja has very little street crime involving handguns, because Mexico banned private ownership of firearms years ago, banned possessing ammunition, and imposed mandatory prison sentences. Of course, bad things do happen. In January 2010, *bandidos* carjacked two cars at gunpoint in downtown Rosarito. Armed carjacking, a new level of crime in town, prompted the mayor to call a town meeting to discuss safety. About 100 people attended. How many USA cities of 100,000 would have a town meeting after bad guys carjacked two vehicles?

Baja also has non-violent street crime. ATM crime happens often in Baja, just as in the USA. It happened to me too. The ATM wouldn't take my card and a Mexican about twenty years old told me in pretty good *inglés* that I was trying to insert it backwards. He grabbed my card, turned it around, and inserted the card for me. I entered my PIN after he was gone. The ATM rejected it and spit out the card. I put on my reading glasses and looked at the card. IT WASN'T MINE. He switched cards so quickly I didn't realize it. At least in Baja, he was trying to get my money with fast fingers rather than using a pistol.

For most stories of things that go wrong in Baja, there are other stories of things that go right. One friend says she accidentally dropped her wallet in a Rosarito store one day and didn't realize it. The store started paging her to come to the service desk. Someone had returned her wallet with all the cash, cards, and IDs intact. Another friend accidentally left his wallet in a Tijuana taxi. He figured all was lost and canceled his cards. The cab driver drove fifteen miles to his house in Rosarito the next day with everything still in the wallet, including a chunk of cash.

As I said in the beginning, most people in Baja know that violent crime almost never touches ordinary citizens, tourists, and expats. When my other attempts fail to persuade friends and family that Baja has relatively little crime, I tell some of them about a popular chain liquor store in downtown Rosarito at the corner of Benito Juarez Boulevard and Magnolia. It has huge glass windows on both streets, almost sixty linear feet of windows, with hundreds of bottles of liquor displayed on shelves just behind the glass.

However, it has no steel bars or wire mesh or anything else to keep thieves from breaking the glass and taking whatever they want. It doesn't have security cameras on the outside of the store, just energy efficient lights to help window shoppers see better.

I wonder how long those windows would last in most USA cities.

Chapter 25:

A Little *Azúcar*

Retiring and spending most of my time in Baja was like starting a new chapter in the book of life.

Certainly, I miss my family and friends back in the USA. Also, coping with problems and the infrastructure in a developing country is sometimes frustrating. However, I adapted to life in Baja and learned how to make *limonada* from *limones,* with a little *azúcar* to make it taste better.

Metaphorically, the *azúcar* comes in the form of many new acquaintances and sharing wonderful experiences with them. It's easy in Baja—Mexicans, Central Americans, South Americans, Europeans, and even Canadians and *Americanos* offer *abrazos,* arm handshakes, and warm smiles. Sometimes I bump into somebody from the old days back in the USA. That's how I met Anna and Doug, who were at dinner one night at La Fonda. She recognized me from working on the same 1971 governor's campaign in Louisiana, after I left journalism.

Many expats share a common bond, finding causes and ways to help those less fortunate, and trying to make life better for others in Baja. Arthur and Molly and Charlie and many others promote annual fund-raising efforts to help fund La Misión public schools. Rosemary and D.J., plus Natalie, Carol, and others, embrace the cause of Casa de Paz orphanage in the *Valle de Guadalupe*.

Gil, who wrote a book about mariachi, helps organize the international mariachi festival in Rosarito to raise money for a new $1.5 million Boys and Girls Club. Peter, another writer and a retired airline pilot, helps poor residents as part of the Flying Samaritans. Dozens of Rosarito expats in the United Society of Baja California help in many other ways, and other expats organize donations to the *Cruz Roja*.

Carla and Jim and others in Bajamar organize charity golf events. By herself, Carlita in Plaza del Mar matches schoolkids back in California with orphans in La Misión to provide bags of Christmas cheer. Ted and Karen help an orphanage north of Rosarito. Debbie and Sandy and others rescue stray dogs and cats, and find homes for them in the USA. There are many more volunteers and do-gooders all around the Baja peninsula.

One of my favorite local causes is the holiday giving organized by La Misión residents as part of *Feliz Navidad*. Dozens of people in the community help, and Arthur relishes the full-dress role of "Santa" he inherited from his father in New York. After distributing Christmas gifts for several years in various locales when he lived in the USA Arthur reprised the role of *"Papá Noel"* in Baja.

Upon my return to Baja in January 2010 after the Christmas holidays, D.J. drafted me immediately to help feed children at Casa de Paz orphanage on Three Kings' Day, the Mexican holiday celebrating the twelfth day of Christmas. Chef Marla of BoutiqueDining.net in San Diego assigned tasks to everyone and gave me a cook's apron to help her batter and fry fifty pounds of fish for tacos. Doug reigned as a king for the day, wearing an elaborate borrowed crown and helping distribute presents that included winter caps knitted by Arthur's sister and mother-in-law.

Los niños crowded around all of us, as hungry for affection as they were for fish tacos. It was a heaping spoonful of *azúcar* and a great way to begin another winter in Baja.

Arthur y Niños—Photo by Nadine Lockitch

D.J. and Bev are major organizers of the La Misión Children's Fund. They created the umbrella group as a 501(c) (3) non-profit in the U.S. with the help of Kathleen, a professor at the University of Southern California who has a house in Playa la Misión. Casa de Paz is a primary focus of the LMCF, along with children who need money for school and families who need help feeding hungry children.

To feed the poor, LMCF recruits others to help with time, money, canned goods, and *frioles y arroz*. Estela at her little grocery in La Misión helps identify the poor, watching for people who search their pockets for pesos to pay for food and come up empty-handed. Across the bridge on the other side of the stream, Oscar in his wheelchair at his little grocery does the same, handing out pieces of paper people can take to the food bank and register for help.

Every Saturday, dozens of poor residents visit the food bank in a little storefront next door to Estela's grocery. Men and women and children line up outside, babies wrapped in blankets, hoping for the weekly sustenance. Some arrive as early as 9 a.m., huddling together and waiting for distribution at 11 a.m. Rosemary greets them and checks names against the list on the pages stuck on her clipboard. Inside, D.J. and Estela and others pass the weekly ration of beans and rice in plastic bags to outstretched hands.

The food bank tries to help poor families stay together in Baja, which isn't always easy. Mexican children from a variety of backgrounds fill orphanages on the edges of towns, on the hills, and across the mountains in the valleys. Some had parents who died. Some have parents who moved to the USA, hoping to build a better life and send for the children to join them someday. Others are unwanted, cast aside by parents and other relatives too poor to feed additional family members, especially those with learning disabilities.

Helping the poor and the orphans is something else we share in Baja in addition to roadtrips, dinners in good restaurants, birthday parties, playing golf and fishing, participating in festivals with music and wine and art and books, and enjoying great live music.

Some days, helping others seems more important than all the rest. Especially on Saturdays when I see the line of people at the food bank, and on Three Kings' Day when *los niños* bless us with their smiles.

Chapter 26:
Green Butter, Earthquakes, and New Wine

After watching whales with "crazy women" in early March of 2010, my next roadtrip was anticlimactic and more mellow. The annual San Felipé blues festival the last weekend in March was fun, and we missed the earthquake in Mexicali by a few days.

You can learn a lot about friends and neighbors on a Baja roadtrip while sharing stories about lost youth, former husbands or wives, and adjusting to living alone. We rolled through the green valleys and into the mountains, heading for the low desert on the other side. A couple of hours into the drive, one of the friends dug into her bag of goodies to share an on-the-go snack with the rest of us. Sections of blood oranges. Cheese. Slices of homemade whole grain bread. Raspberry jam. There was also something called "green butter," which she said I couldn't have because I was driving. She has a medical marijuana card.

We found our rental house at the El Dorado Ranch and headed to the ballpark downtown for the blues festival. Maria Elena and her poodle Sammy walked around a lot. Scott and Lupé and Rosemary danced sometimes. Georgiann and I were content to mostly sit and listen. Many other friends and neighbors were there from Rosarito, La Misión, and Ensenada, including Rosella's mother Alicia and her husband Sergio. The crowd swelled to 600 or so by early evening.

Rosemary came back from visiting the long row of portable toilets separated by gender and reported to Georgiann about the conditions. We all laughed as she described women telling other women in line which porta-potties were best. Clean. Dirty. Plenty of paper. Out of paper. We laughed more at her observation that the one she visited had the unmistakable aroma of marijuana.

"Some ladies are enjoying a little pot in the potty," she said.

All the bands were good. Becki Sue & Her Big Rockin' Daddies were outstanding. She came down from the stage holding a wireless microphone, wearing red shoes with stiletto heels, shaking her booty inside a white mini-dress, and wailing about a bad case of the blues. Dozens of dancers crowded around her, snapping digital pix and shooting videos. Together, they stomped the sandy infield into dust the desert wind swirled around people sitting close by. That included us. All six of us suffered from breathing too much desert dust—we coughed and sneezed through the night.

Most of us felt better the next morning after some herbal tea. We headed into town looking for a church where Lupé could satisfy her spiritual hunger on Palm Sunday. After dropping her off at a nice *iglesia*, we satisfied our appetites over lunch at a *loncheria*. Scott and I went back to get her and found her standing out front.

"*No fue bueno,*" she said, disappointed that it wasn't as good as she expected.

She had found a good seat in a pew close to the front. After a few minutes sitting alone she had realized almost everybody else was in the side courtyard. The priest spent twenty-five minutes blessing palm fronds, stripping off palm leaves, and giving them to worshipers to tie into little crosses. Re-entering the church with everyone else, she found an elderly woman had taken her seat and was saving several places. The woman refused to give her a place although Lupé explained she was sitting there earlier.

"So?" the old woman told her.

After we checked out of the rental house, Scott, Lupé, Maria Elena, and Sammy decided to hang out on the *Malécon* jammed with spring breakers. We older folks headed for the tiny village of Puertecitos about forty miles south. Rosemary knew about a natural hot springs right on the Sea of Cortez and said it wasn't too hard to find. We just followed the good road until it ended, turned left toward the water, and took the bad road over the rocky ridge. There it was. The tide was going out, exposing tidal pools along the rocky shoreline, each one warmed by the natural hot springs.

Puertecitos Hot Springs

Debra, a neighbor of Rosemary, was soaking in one of the tidal pools with her new man Sam. He was looking trim after having a gastric bypass operation in Mexico to curb his appetite and losing 120 pounds. We decided to stay overnight back in town because it was getting too late to drive home across the mountains before dark. Debra recommended a restaurant that featured the famous San Felipé shrimp, and we passed up the chance to eat at a roadside cafe named Cow Patty. Maybe next year.

We took the long way home to La Misión the next morning, heading North from San Felipé to the capital city of Mexicali and then across to Tecate. During the two hours enroute to Mexicali, Georgiann and Rosemary took turns giving me a history lesson on the Chinese immigration in the early 1900s. We stopped for a midday meal at one of the dozens of Chinese restaurants in *La Chinesca*, the Chinese section of the city. The scenic 4,000-foot high mountain pass between Mexicali and Tecate was a beautiful drive, a steep ascent up red rock mountains pushed skyward by geological forces perhaps two million years ago.

The epicenter of the major earthquake[37] south of Mexicali the following Sunday was just twelve miles east of our route between San Felipé and Mexicali. It triggered more than 100 aftershocks in the area of several fault lines[38] between the San Andreas Fault system in Southern California through the Imperial Valley to the Sea of Cortez. (During the earthquake, I felt the shaking more than 100 miles away in Rosarito for nearly a minute.)

Three weeks later, I had my last roadtrip of the spring. It was a short day trip to the *Valle de Guadalupe* for an art festival and wine tasting at La Casa Vieja, owned by Humberto and Colleen near Ensenada. Arthur, Molly, and Rosemary carpooled with me, along with Jacki who took some of her art to exhibit. The midday fog made its way up the mountains from the shoreline – "on little cat feet" Molly recalled that Carl Sandburg wrote – and curled up on the slopes overlooking the valley.

Several other friends from the La Misión area were there, including Jack and his dog named Blue. We saw some

[37] http://en.wikipedia.org/wiki/2010_Baja_California_earthquake
[38] http://www.uoregon.edu/~rdorsey/LagSal.html

quality art and sculpture, enjoyed Argentine-style cooking from the outdoor grill, and listened to a classical guitar player. Joanna and her dance partner demonstrated intricate Tango moves. Her new wine won first place in the blind tasting and she promised to start pouring it at her *Galeria y Café* in the summer. On the way home, Arthur read a new scene from his screenplay about Garry Davis and world peace. He and I laughed at the irony of reading it while waiting at a Mexican military checkpoint.

For me, a roadtrip in Baja is a feel-good potpourri. Some of my trips are for a few days or a few weeks; others are for a single day. Some trips focus on lagoons and whales; others explore mountains and seacoasts. Some feature blues music and hot springs; others have art and new wine. All of them include good friends.

Already, some of my friends and I are planning another trip—to the observatory on top of that Baja mountain 9,000 feet in the sky. Some people say you can have a religious experience up there; others say it's just the lack of oxygen. On a clear night, they say, you can see every constellation in the sky from up there. On a clear day, others tell me, you can watch the sun emerge from the Sea of Cortez at dawn, arc across the mountain sky, and disappear into the Pacific Ocean at dusk.

I want to see that too.

I Love Baja!

Chapter 27:
They Took The Street

After a trip to the states, I headed back to Baja in September 2010. Rosella met me at my U.S. mailbox just north of the border and filled me in on the latest happenings.

"There is good news, Mr. Miller—they're making a concrete street in front of your house," she said as we neared the *casita* in Rosarito I rented from her mother in February. I agreed that was great, because I always hated when rains turned the one-block dirt street into impassable mud going up the hill.

"There is also bad news," she said. "The road machinery broke the water pipe to your house and you have no water. I am sorry."

"*No hay problema*," I told her, remembering my reserve of two twenty-litre water jugs. She rolled to a stop on a street across the vacant lot from my place. I wondered why.

"There is more," she said. "They took the street."

Before I could ask what that meant, Mexican neighbors appeared in the early darkness. They formed a procession to carry my suitcase, computer bag, book bag, and two cardboard boxes of books and clothing. I followed them on the dusty footpath through the vacant lot, stepping around rocks and debris, until we reached the edge of my street. Sure enough, it was gone.

Street After Excavation, With SUV Behind Gate

All that remained was a dirt ditch, about thirty inches below where the dirt street surface used to be. Piles of loose dirt blocked my descent. I held onto the hand of a stout neighbor whose name I didn't know, scrambled over one pile, and slipped and skidded down the loose dirt and debris into what was left of the street. My housekeeper and her husband were waiting on the other side. He reached for me and pulled me out of the ditch, onto the end of the driveway. My trusty SUV sat marooned behind the padlocked gate.

"Maybe you'll have water tomorrow," Rosella said. "Maybe they will make the concrete soon."

People from the water company repaired the broken water pipe late the next day. The road crew foreman said yes, the street would be ready within a week. My walk around the neighborhood on the weekend discovered many streets under construction. However, the paving equipment was nowhere in sight. It still hadn't arrived on Tuesday. In fact, no road workers of any kind were around. I asked Rosella to check on what was happening.

"There are big problems," she said an hour or so later. "The water pipes under the street are bad, and they are deciding what to do. They cannot make the concrete until they decide." I asked how long that might be.

"Ah, that is not easy to say. Tomorrow is the day before Mexican Independence Day, when people gather in the evening to hear government officials deliver *el grito* before midnight," she continued. "Then Thursday is Independence Day, which is a national holiday, with a parade. And the workers have off on Friday because this year is the 200th anniversary of independence."

"But I need to go to La Misión this next weekend to see people," I told her. "There's a birthday party I don't want to miss, plus dinner with friends."

"Yes, yes, I will see what I can do," she replied.

Family and friends back in the USA laughed at my email description of the situation, especially the photo I sent to them showing where the street used to be. Some suggested solutions, such as buying metal ramps. I decided to trust Rosella, not wanting to offend her by trying my own remedies. Besides, I had faith in her, remembering how she had solved many problems for me since my arrival nearly three years earlier.

Wednesday came and went. The next morning Rosella invited me to walk over to her house nearby to have *desayuno* with a guy from city hall. I didn't understood what his job was, but he was driving a new Ford Explorer that belonged to the city. The three of us chatted about the Independence Day parade scheduled later that morning.

I'd learned over time to keep quiet and let Rosella work her magic on people. She cooked a skillet full of *papas, chorizo,* and *huevos*, and stuffed a dozen soft flour tortilla shells with the great smelling mixture. Chopped vegetables and garnish rounded out the meal, plus fresh mangoes. The blender produced a great-tasting smoothie of bananas and chocolate milk, a favorite treat for her kids. The guy from city hall and I liked it too.

He finished his fourth taco and pushed back his plate, and I could sense Rosella was ready to make her move.

"*Por favor*, what is the news about the water pipes?" she asked him. "It's been a week now, and nothing is happening yet."

"Such decisions are not easy," he said. "Three weeks; not more."

"But Mr. Miller has meetings on Saturday, and his car cannot get out because the street is gone." She moved closer to him and touched his arm. "Is there anything you can do?"

"I will check to see," he replied.

"*Muchas gracias*," I said, recognizing my cue. "Whatever you can do would be great." I shook his hand, excused myself, and wished them well at the parade.

Later in the afternoon, I heard noises on the street in front of my *casita* and looked out. The same guy was out there with a shovel and a wheelbarrow. He was wearing work boots, cutoffs and a T-shirt, filling the wheelbarrow with dirt from the piles across the street. It was almost unbelievable. Rosella was smiling and watching her seven-year-old son José Carlos wield a little shovel of his own.

I joined the impromptu work crew, taking turns shoveling one load after another, piling dirt against the end of my driveway to build a ramp. After we filled and dumped about fifteen loads, I backed the SUV into the street. We slapped high-fives, and he returned the wheelbarrow and shovel to one of the neighbors.

Two weeks dragged on without any sign of progress on the street. The dirt ditch where the street used to be became hard and packed by neighborhood traffic weaving around the exposed manhole covers.

In the third week, the city decided to replace the water pipes, just as the guy had predicted.

In the fourth week, workers used backhoe equipment to dig water ditches throughout the neighborhood and install new pipes.

In the fifth week, dump trucks arrived on the next street over, depositing piles of gravel for the new roadbed. Road graders smoothed the piles. I watched their progress with optimism, knowing my street would be next.

In the sixth week, the rains came.

It rained for three nights and three days—a relentless rain, torrential and pounding hour after hour, unusual for Baja in late October. I stayed inside the *casita* until early Wednesday morning, when I needed to go to the weekly meeting with other writers. Unfortunately, I had left the SUV parked near the bottom of the hill, on the low side of the ditch where the street used to be. It was standing in a pond up to the running boards.

In such situations, even a SUV is no match for Mexican mud. It refuses to turn loose a vehicle mired in the bottom of a shallow pond, encases the tires in goop, and turns them into spinning wheels. It also tries to suck the boots from your feet. I hitched a ride to downtown with Rosella when she left for work, abandoning hope for the SUV until Mother Nature drained the pond.

The rain stopped later that afternoon. Thursday was partly cloudy, and Friday and Saturday were partly sunny. The pond shrank a little. Friends advised me to get the SUV out before the sun dried the pond completely and turned the mud hole into adobe, which might enshrine the SUV as a monument to gringo stupidity. Not to worry—it rained again Sunday night and into the next morning, adding more water to the pond.

On Wednesday morning, I flagged down a propane gas delivery truck in the neighborhood and had it pull the SUV out of the mud. The driver accepted a *propina* of $5, almost a day's wages, and both of us were happy. I drove to a car wash, flinging chunks of mud in a trail for blocks.

Doug and Anna offered to let me rent their oceanfront cabana in Plaza del Mar for the winter, and I moved away from the little street before the rainy season began in earnest. Just before a trip to Maryland for the Christmas holidays, I drove back to the neighborhood in Rosarito to check on the progress.

Thirteen weeks after the road crew took the street away, there was still no sign of concrete work. Neighbors in the three other houses on the same block had adapted to their fate, building dirt ramps from the ditch to their own driveways.

Mexicans may have difficulty dealing with big issues such as the economy, drug cartels, oil exploration, and the education system. Replacing water pipes and completing concrete streets also pose challenges. But the people are great at solving individual problems with a human touch.

I still marvel at what the guy from city hall did to help me during the bicentennial celebration of Independence Day. I wonder if there's a city official anywhere in the USA who would interrupt a national holiday celebration, borrow a wheelbarrow, and shovel dirt with his own hands to help a foreigner.

Of course, city officials back in the states have never met Rosella.

Epilogue

I enjoy writing about Baja as much as I like living here.

However, I don't think I want to grow old alone in a foreign country with my closest kin thousands of miles away. Fathers and sons and grandsons should spend more time together. Maybe I'll spend winters and summers in Baja, and spend other months with family and friends in the USA.

Some people who reviewed the 2009 manuscript suggested that it needed appendices about the cost of living on the Baja Gold Coast and medical care in Mexico. Other reviewers said I should include information about real estate risks in Mexico. I added those two appendices, plus a section at the end of the book on real estate risks. Thanks to the many people who reviewed these additions.

I welcome feedback on the book, and I look forward to writing more about life in Baja—perhaps even a sequel someday.

~ Mikel Miller, Baja California, Mexico, June 2011

I Love Baja!

Appendix A:
Affordable Retirement

If you are trying to find an affordable and accommodating place to retire, consider the Baja Gold Coast of Mexico from Rosarito to Ensenada.

The northwest Pacific Coast of Baja has rugged cliffs and sweeping ocean vistas, like the Big Sur area of California, and enough sand and surf to please almost everybody from beachcombers to surfers. Moreover, many locals speak good English.

By the fall of 2008, the cost of living became very affordable in this area—less than half what it would cost in the USA for a similar lifestyle. In addition, the exchange rate of Mexican pesos to U.S. dollars makes money go further. My own experiences and those of other expats confirm this. If you want independent confirmation, one of the best sources of information on Baja retirement is a recent comprehensive study by the International Community Foundation.[39] The ICF has several scholarly reports on retirement living in Mexico.

Housing offers good value and, in the winter of 2009-2010, a wide range of individual houses or condos was

---

[39] http://www.icfdn.org/publications/retireeresearch/

available. Prices on many existing residences in expatriate communities with other USA and Canadian citizens plunged during the real estate bust beginning in 2008, and many are fully furnished. Similar properties on the USA Pacific coast still cost several times as much, even after the real estate crash. Monthly HOA maintenance fees average about $100-$150 in upscale communities but were far less in other communities.

Playa Salsipuedes North of Ensenada

Rental housing starts at about $200 a month, and a two-bedroom place costs less than $500 a month, usually with utilities included. Asking prices in upscale communities could be twice that much, but they are negotiable. In some predominately-Mexican communities, purchase prices and rentals are lower still.

Almost all expatriate communities are gated; most have 24/7 security by uniformed *seguridados*. Many communities have one or more pools, a Jacuzzi, picnic and playground areas.

Utilities are relatively inexpensive, compared with USA climates that require extensive air conditioning and heat. With average daytime high temperatures in the sixties and seventies all year, homes do not need air conditioning, and newer residences use economical gas heat. A typical monthly bill for electric, gas, water, and sewer averages between $100-$125—less if you conserve.

Property taxes are very low. Property taxes for a $200,000-$400,000 residence in this area are $250-$300 annually. Residents over sixty pay only half that much, or about $12.50 a month, if they register at the tax office and pay directly rather than using an agent.

The Mexican bank trust annual fee for a $200,000-$400,000 property is $500 or less. Having a bank trust, or *fideicomiso*, is the only way a foreigner can own real estate legally in Baja. In essence, Mexico transfers the property rights to the buyer, and a local bank holds the deed in a trust.

Groceries and food have bargain prices. Two people can eat very well for less than $200 monthly. Most expatriates use discounted pesos for fresh fruit and vegetables, meat, staples, and household goods at Calimax, Comercial Mexicana, Costco, or Wal-Mart. Meat bargains are in neighborhood *carnicerias* that cut NY strip steaks to order for only $4 a pound. Two pounds of jumbo shrimp are only $9 at *el mercado de mariscos* on the Ensenada waterfront. Live California spiny lobsters from *los pescadores* at the Popotla fishing village are less than $10 per pound. Refilling a twenty-litre bottle with purified water costs less than $1.

Dining out offers good value for the money. Two people can enjoy dining out at least once a week for less than $25, or about $100 a month, including Margaritas. Most restaurants offer full dinners ranging from $8-$14 for meat or seafood dishes, with generous portions two people can share. Two lobster tails at the Puerto Nuevo lobster village cost about $16. Even at an upscale French restaurant in Ensenada, most entrees are only $9-$19, half what the same entrees cost almost anywhere in the USA. Many restaurants have two-for-one drink specials and early-bird-special full meals for $4-$7 between 4-7 p.m.

Leisure time activities cost less. Ticket prices are low for museums, cultural events, and festivals. Current English-language movies in a new movie cineplex cost less than $3 on Wednesdays. At Bajamar, local residents pay less than $40 for eighteen holes of golf after 1 o'clock, including a cart, with four holes over crashing ocean surf. A half-day offshore fishing trip is $25.

Miscellaneous expenses are reasonable. About $70 monthly covers all of these—the annual Mexican immigration documents, mandatory auto liability insurance from a Mexican insurance company, homeowner's insurance, a private postal service, and maybe a bill paying service.

Most personal services are inexpensive. A visit to the doctor or dentist costs $25 or less. Prescription drugs often cost less than the co-pay in the USA. Several spas offer discounts to people who sign up for resident cards. Haircuts are $5-$7.

The bottom line appears to be that living in Baja can cost much less than living in the USA. Much of that cost difference is due to low property taxes, reduced expenses for heat and air conditioning, and inexpensive medical care. In November of 2008, I began tracking my expenses weekly and learned my annual monthly living costs averaged less than $1,000 for the following basic categories:

- Monthly rental (w/ utilities) $500
- Groceries 120
- Dining out 100
- Gasoline and tolls 100
- Leisure time activities 100
- Miscellaneous 50

Of course, you can spend a lot more if you travel a lot or eat in places that cater to *turistas* with pricey food and drink menus. A few expatriates they say spend almost as much on dining out and leisure activities in Baja as they did back in their homelands. Also, customs on foreign products sold in Baja stores - such as appliances, computers, TVs - can increase costs.

Shopping offers great bargains. Residents can watch local artisans hand paint Mexican tiles for their homes, and order custom-built wood and iron furniture for a fraction of the cost in the USA. Original art, fine silver, sculpture, and ceramics from local artists are available in dozens of galleries and shops at very reasonable prices.

Anything residents miss about the USA is only a short drive away. Many area expatriates drive to San Diego frequently for doctor visits, banking, shopping, or other errands, and are back home for dinner. San Diego, the ninth largest U.S. city, offers professional sports teams, opera and symphony performances, the world famous San Diego Zoo, historic Old Town, Little Italy, and the San Diego harbor. It also has plenty of direct flights to cities across the USA and to Canada.

The air quality and climate are very good, with fresh air from unpolluted northwesterly winds sweeping across the Pacific Ocean. The climate is much like coastal San Diego—mostly sunny, not too cold, and not too hot. The humidity is usually a comfortable sixty percent, and the only significant rainfall is about two inches a month from late November to early March. Sometimes, fog and ocean mist blanket the shoreline until late morning and again in the evening.

All retirees need to find an affordable and accommodating place to enjoy retirement. For me, this is the place.

I Love Baja!

Appendix B:

Mexican Health Care

The overall quality of major health care in Mexico is as good as many places in the USA. Herb, a retired physician from San Francisco, says he is impressed with medical school training in Mexico, particularly at the University in Mexico City.

One of the best sources of information about health care in Mexico for U.S. citizens is a May 2010 report by the International Community Foundation.[40] Another article[41] on medical tourism states "The cost of medical and dental procedures in Mexico is, on average, about 25 to 50 percent of U.S. costs." Some major procedures offer greater savings. A hip replacement costing $100,000 in the USA costs only $12,000 in one of these facilities, according to the article.

All of this helps explain why international medical tourism for USA residents is a growing industry in Mexico, as well as other countries. One study[42] by Deloitte Center for Health Solutions states the actual number of U.S. citizens

---

[40] http://www.icfdn.org/publications/healthcare/index.php
[41] "Mexico Living", October 2009, p. 10
[42] http://www.deloitte.com/assets/Dcom-UnitedStates/Local%20Assets/Documents/us_chs_MedicalTourism_102609.pdf

traveling outside the USA for medical care in 2008 was 540,000, down from 750,000 in 2007 before the recession. However, the same study estimates 648,000 in 2009 and a "recession-adjusted forecast" for 1.6 million by the end 2012. Mexico is an attractive destination, with short travel times and many vacation options.

Just as in other countries, not every medical outcome in Mexico is perfect. Two expatriates told me of cases that required second opinions in the USA and follow-up surgery. But these are exceptions to the otherwise high quality of private health care in Mexico.

In essence, Mexico has three tiers of health care. I base this on talking with other expatriates and Mexicans, discussing coverage with medical providers, reading print articles, and researching on the Internet. Some of my general information came from very informative articles in 2007-2009 in *Mexico Living*, a publication focusing on Northwest Mexico and based in San Felipé.

- The first tier provides a safety net of very limited medical treatment for people who become ill and can afford to pay little or nothing.
- A second tier, run by the Mexican national health care system through the Mexican Institute of Social Security (IMSS), offers broad coverage in public clinics and hospitals. This relatively affordable medical insurance program covers doctors and dentists, including free medicine, with no deductibles, at over 1,500 clinics and 250 hospitals. Foreign residents can enroll in the IMSS medical care program, which requires a physical exam and lots of identification papers. It excludes some serious preexisting conditions, but it covers most illness and surgeries after an initial waiting period, covers more in the second year, and almost everything else in the third year.

- On the third tier, private practice health care providers and private hospitals provide personalized services to residents who can afford to pay for it. Some people prefer to use private doctors and facilities for their routine health care needs, but say they enrolled in IMSS as protection against catastrophic medical needs.

As in the United States, it isn't always easy to sort through the details of international health care coverage and find the cost of premiums. Some Internet sources provide information about health care coverage in Mexico. One is www.MedToGo.com, and another is www.MexConnect.com. Also, author Julia Taylor has a good book, "*Mexico: The Trick Is Living Here*," and further information on her website at www.home-sweet-mexico.com.

Private doctors in Baja rarely accept USA medical insurance coverage, or credit cards or checks. Therefore, patients pay cash and then can seek reimbursement from USA insurance plans, sometimes with success. According to some articles, a few private Mexican hospitals are beginning to accept American health insurance coverage. Other reports speculate that U.S. insurance companies and private Mexican health care providers will try to work out mechanisms to make it easier for patients to pay for medical care in Mexico.

Foreigners can also buy international or Mexican private insurance. Premiums are generally lower than USA insurance plan - usually less than $1,000 a year - but enrollees usually have to pay annual premiums in advance. After patients meet requirements for annual deductibles, these insurance plans usually pay all remaining costs. The plans require a physical, but some indicate they might accept a letter from a personal physician attesting to no preexisting conditions. Velmar Hospital in Ensenada has a desk in the lobby for the insurance company GNP to offer coverage.

As you might expect, entrepreneurs are looking at all the aging Baby Boomers in the USA and seeing an excellent opportunity to cash in on medical tourism in Mexico. In the summer of 2009, some health care providers in Southern California and Northern Baja banded together and began promoting a cross-border medical practice.

Some reports say Mexican billionaire Carlos Slim, as rich or richer than Bill Gates, plans to diversify into upscale private hospitals that will cater to USA Boomers. According to one report in the San Diego *Union-Tribune*,[43] one of his projects might be in Tijuana.

As of the end of 2009, U.S. citizens still could not use Medicare hospital benefits in Mexico. Some expats say the new health care legislation passed in 2010 allows Medicare Part D payments for prescription drugs in Mexico; others aren't so sure. For now, most Medicare recipients travel back to the USA for major health needs. That's what I plan to do, if I develop a major problem requiring lengthy hospitalization. In addition, as a federal government retiree, I have an affordable group insurance policy that covers most physician treatment in the USA as long as I maintain U.S. residency requirements.

Some folks are even lobbying the U.S. Congress, trying to extend Medicare coverage for people who want to travel to Mexico for health care. The same *Union-Tribune* article reported Mexico is urging the USA to allow Medicare benefits for medical care in Mexico. The November 2009 issue of *International Living* reported the chief executive officer of Promexico, Mexico's foreign investment agency, believes the governments of Mexico and the U.S. might have an agreement by 2011 to let Americans use Medicare and Medicaid insurance at Mexican health care facilities. Part of his optimism is that it could help curtail rising Medicare costs in the USA.

---

[43] http://www.signonsandiego.com/news/2010/apr/21/mexican-health-care-for-americans-studied/

There are many laws, regulations, and bureaucratic rules governing what happens when a foreigner dies in Mexico, just as in the USA. Procedures in Mexico are different depending on whether death occurs in a hospital, at home, or in an accident somewhere. Authorities often override personal and religious preferences regarding autopsy, embalming, and cremation. At a minimum, just in case, foreigners should arrange for a personal physician in Mexico, a mortuary, and a *Notario*. Planning is critical and should include registering with the foreign Consulate. Even with planning, most foreign deaths in Mexico involve lengthy police interviews, removing the body to the government morgue, and embalming.

Foreigners should have a *Notario* prepare a Certificate of Ratification, which can cut through much of the Mexican bureaucracy surrounding death. The document must be *en español*, certified and legally filed by a *Notario*. An immigration professional or a company like Serena can arrange all of this. If a personal physician is able to certify the cause of death at home or in a hospital, this document may bypass the coroner and an autopsy.

If the Certificate of Ratification specifies a mortuary, this may bypass the government morgue. The mortuary can obtain the necessary permits to send the body to another country for burial or facilitate cremation and transport the ashes. Even with the Certificate of Ratification, next-of-kin must provide specific documents to prove relationship to settle a foreigner's estate—a birth certificate, driver's license, passport, and any documents with name changes such as marriage certificates and divorce decrees. All of this is more critical if the next-of-kin is unable to travel to Mexico immediately after your death.

Many people I know in Baja prefer to have their remains taken back to their homeland. The total cost may be $4,000 US or more before your next-of-kin can get your body or ashes out of the country, and transportation may require assistance from a foreign consulate. I want to avoid that hassle. If I die in Baja, my Certificate of Ratification authorizes Rosella to arrange to cremate my body, store my ashes in a little box, and hold onto it for my next-of-kin.

I've also suggested that my sons back in the states use the opportunity to arrange a family roadtrip to watch *las ballenas gris* and help me swim with the whales.

Just as *Papá* did.

Bonus Section:
Real Estate Risks

This section is a brief overview of how to manage risks involving Baja real estate. A more comprehensive discussion of real estate in Mexico is on the Internet in a report published by the International Community Foundation. [44]

I circulated the draft of this section to more than thirty people throughout the Baja peninsula for comment. More than twenty of these are real estate agents, real estate attorneys, developers, closing agents, and principals in title search firms. The others are expat friends and neighbors who invested in Baja real estate.

Some Baja real estate professionals who reviewed the draft complained it might discourage potential real estate buyers. I take the view the section might encourage potential buyers to be more diligent. Others suggested that I shorten the checklist. Paul Clark, a prominent developer near Cabo Pulmo on the East Cape in *Baja California Sur*, said: "Very few of your points can be disputed, but you are making the process too complicated for any novice to follow." He suggested distilling the list to the first five points below:

---

[44] www.icfdn.org/publications/housing/index.php

1. <u>Be pragmatic and not emotional in your purchase.</u>
2. <u>Make certain your money goes into a bonded independent escrow account.</u> Do not give anyone any money in a real estate transaction unless you are giving it to a bonded escrow agency. Read and understand the bond/surety that will protect your money. Many real estate agents and developers in Mexico do not put your money into a protected escrow account. Your money may disappear before you know it.
3. <u>Find a good English speaking *Notario* with good references.</u> In Mexico the only person who can legally transfer property is a *Notario*. Transfer of money from the escrow account only happens on transfer of legal title and possession of the property.
4. <u>Translate all paperwork to English.</u>
5. <u>Buy only property that is ready for occupancy</u>—what you see is what you get. If you are making deposits or accepting property that is not completed, you are financing the developer—probably because traditional financing to complete the project was not available. If you really want to buy into a new project, make certain your money goes to escrow until completion and transfer of title.

I believe buyers should never proceed with a Mexican real estate purchase or make payments without taking actions to manage risks covered by these five points. The following additional points are also worth considering:

1. Insist on obtaining a legal *fideicomiso,* or bank trust. This is the only legal way a foreigner can own real estate within the restricted zone in Mexico.

2. Consider using a real estate agent who belongs to an organization of real estate professionals. As of early 2010, Mexico didn't have licensing requirements for real estate agents. However, it had two organizations of real estate professionals—AMPI and API—both of which have standards and codes of ethics and sanctions.

3. Try to use a real estate attorney who is independent from the seller.

4. Make sure your representatives check for liens and other hidden issues. Even if the land has a clear title, liens on it may prevent the seller from transferring the rights to you. Without these rights, you cannot obtain a *fideicomiso*.

5. Include an arbitration clause in any contract. Based on provisions in NAFTA, Mexico modified its laws to permit voluntary Alternative Dispute Resolution and has provided for enforcement of arbitration awards in the courts. This may allow you to resolve disputes without a lawsuit, and it may resolve differences within a few months after filing a complaint.

6. Consider obtaining title insurance from a reputable title insurance firm.

7. To further protect your interests in a real estate transaction, consider hiring an independent professional closing agent as a neutral third party to facilitate the process.

8. Create and file a legal Mexican Power of Attorney (POA) form. You need a Mexican POA naming someone who can act on your behalf in Baja if you become incapacitated, especially in real estate matters. The POA is ONLY valid while the grantor is alive. A Mexican POA is based on specific provisions

in the Mexican Civil Code and you should get a model POA from a Mexican Consulate. *Notarios* must approve a POA and file it with the public records office for it to be legal.

9. Be aware of capital gains tax traps when obtaining the *fideicomiso*. Some sellers try to reduce their taxes by low-balling the appraised value in legal documents, which creates a higher capital gains tax liability for the buyer.

10. Prepare and file a legal Mexican will. Just as in the USA, Mexican courts can drag out the inheritance process and make it difficult for your heirs if you do not have a will. A *Notario* can create your Mexican will for under $200 US.

11. Consider simplifying your life by arranging for a professional firm to monitor and pay the annual fee for your Mexican bank trust. Mexican banks charge an annual fee for administering your *fideicomiso*, usually under $500 US. The best way to avoid the hassle and make sure you pay on time is to hire a professional firm to do this for you. Some of these firms also handle payments for utilities, taxes, and other matters.

12. Understand the tax laws in Mexico and the USA that apply to real estate in Mexico, especially the difference between capital gains and income. Consult a reputable international tax attorney, because the tax laws in both countries change frequently.

13. Be aware of IRS requirements in the USA for annual reporting of the *fideicomiso*. Information is available online.[45]

---

[45] http://www.irs.gov/businesses/international/article/0,,id=185295,00.html

I want to thank two people in particular who vetted this section. One is Linda Neil from La Paz, a recognized international authority on Mexican real estate. Her website is http://www.settlement-co.com/. The other is Ross Buck from Rosarito, president of First Title Services and a leader among real estate professionals in northern Baja. His website is http://www.1sttitleservices.com/. Linda also suggests people read *"The Complete Guide to Buying a Second Home or Real Estate in Mexico,"* a comprehensive 2010 book by Jackie Bondanza. Other books also include sections on Baja real estate, including the 2010 edition of *"Good Info For Gringos Living in Baja,"* by Peter Fowler.

One Baja real estate agent denounced the additional points in my checklist, saying, "You're trying to impose the USA way of doing real estate." Two other agents said there is no need for potential buyers to worry about all these risks because Mexico has many laws to protect against fraud. The report by the International Community Foundation makes it clear these laws do not protect the rights of foreigners in real estate transactions. Moreover, it is unlikely the Mexican justice system will get the buyer's money back—remember the project with Donald Trump's name on it.

Most checklist reviewers in Baja agree it's a good basic guide to managing real estate risks. However, some say, "You don't really need to do all those things." A few scoff at some of my additional points saying, "Nobody does that."

Hmmmm. That's a little like ignoring the *Alto* traffic signs in Mexico—everybody knows the signs mean stop. Hardly anyone comes to a full stop in Baja, however, including foreigners. Usually, a quick look or rolling stop works just fine. But you are risking a lot if something bad happens because you don't obey that *Alto* sign.

The same is true of failing to heed potential risks when investing in Mexican real estate.

I Love Baja!

Glossary

Some words and phrases en español in Mexico are slightly different than in Central America, South America, or Spain. Here's a glossary to help you understand what locals are saying in Baja.

¡de nada! – you're welcome

¡Feliz Cumpleaños! – Happy Birthday

¡Feliz Navidad! – Happy Christmas

abolladura – dent (noun)

abrazo – a hug

abuela, abuelo – grandmother, grandfather

abuelita, abuelito – grandma, grandpa

aceite de oliva – olive oil

advertencia – a warning

agosto – August

agua – water

agua purificada – purified water

Aguinaldo – bonus payment

Alto – high, higher (adverb, adjective); also used on all stop signs as a noun

amarillo - yellow
ambulancia - ambulance
amiga de confianza - trusted female friend
amo - I love (verb)
amor - to love (noun)
arreglo - repair (noun)
arroyo - stream
arroz - rice
atún - tuna
auditorio – auditorium
azúcar – sugar
azul – blue
bahía – bay
baile – dance
baja (mas abajo) – lower
Baja California – state of northern Baja California
Baja California Sur – state of southern Baja California
ballena – whale
baño – bathroom
basura – rubbish, garbage, refuse
beso – kiss (noun)
bienvenidos – welcome
blanco – white
bonito – pretty
caballo – horse
cabo – cape
cabra – goat
cachorra, cachorro – puppy (female, male)
café – coffee
café Mexicano – Mexican coffee
caliente – hot
camarones – shrimp
campo – campground
cangrejos – crabs
capas de polvo – layers of dust
carne – meat
carne asada – roasted meat

carnicería – butcher shop
carretera – road
carro – car
casado – married
casita – small house
catorce – 14
cena – evening meal
cero – zero
ceviche mariscos – chopped seafood on a flat taco
chorizo – pork sausage flavored with chile and garlic
churros – fried dough pastry snacks
cielo – sky
cien, ciento – 100
cinco – five
cincuenta – 50
ciudad – the city
clínica – medical clinic
Coca Light – Diet Coke
cocina – kitchen
cojones – testicles
comida – food, mid-day meal
comisaría – police station
computadora – computer
¿cómo estás? – how are you?
con – with
crema – cream
cruz – cross
Cruz Roja – Red Cross
cuarenta – 40
cuatro – four
curva peligroso – dangerous curve
declaración – declaration
delicioso – delicious
delincuente – criminal
desayuno – morning meal, breakfast
desierto – desert
día – day

diciembre – December
dieciésis – 16
diecinueve – 19
dieciocho – 18
diecisiete – 17
diez – 10
dinero – money
Dios - God
disculpe (also) *disculpeme* – excuse me
doble – double
doce – 12
domingo – Sunday
dónde? – where?
efectivo – cash. *Retirar efectivo del banco* - withdraw cash
from a bank
Ejido – communal
El Grito – the shouted war cry to commemorate September
16, the start of the Mexican War of Independence from Spain
eléctrico – electrical
electricista – electrician
enero – January
enfermo – ill
ensalada – salad
éste, ésta – this one
español – Spanish
Estados Unidos de América – United States of America
farmácia – pharmacy
febrero – February
federales – federal police
fideicomiso – a real estate bank trust
fresas – strawberries
fresco – cool temperature
frijoles y arroz – beans and rice
frío – cold
fruta – fruit
fútbol – soccer
ganado – cattle

gata, gato – cat (female, male)
gigante – huge
grande – big
granero – a store with feed and supplies for animals
gratis – free
gringo – slang for a North American not from Mexico
gris – gray
habla – speak
hamburguesa – *hamburger*
hamburguesa con queso – cheeseburger
hasta – until
hasta luego – so long; see you later
hija, hijo – daughter, son
hola – hello
hombre, hombres – man, men
hora – hour
hoy – today
huevo, huevos – egg, eggs
huevos estrellados – fried eggs, cooked on both sides
iglesia – church
inglés – English
instrucciones – instructions
isla – island
jueves – Thursday
juez – the judge
jugo – juice
jugo de naranja – orange juice
julio – July
junio – June
kilo – kilo (measure); equal to 2.2 pounds
la cuenta, por favor – the check, please
la policía; el policía – police, policewoman; policeman
laguna – lagoon
langostas – lobsters
Las Mañanitas – traditional Mexican celebration song
lechuga – lettuce
libro – book

licores – liquor
limón – lemon
limonada – lemonade
lindo – beautiful, pretty
llantas – tires
llantera – tire shop
llave – key
loco – crazy
lunes – Monday
machismo – attitude based on male virility or gender superiority
madre – mother
magnífico –- magnificent
Malécon – waterfront walkway
mano – hand
manzana – apple
mañana – tomorrow
mar – sea
Mar de Cortez – Sea of Cortez
mariscos – seafood
martes – Tuesday
marzo – March
mayo – May
mayonésa – mayonnaise
mecánico – mechanic
médica, médico – doctor (female, male)
mejor – better
mercado – market
mercado de mariscos – fish market
mes – month
mesa – table
mesera – waitress
mi casa es su casa – my house is your house
mi, mis – my (singular, plural)
miércoles – Wednesday
mil – thousand (count)
mole sauce – traditional spicy chocolate sauce

mordida – a small bribe (literally "little bite")
mosca – fly (noun)
motocicleta – motorcycle
mucha, mucho – many
muchacho – kid
muchas gracias – many thanks
muchos saludos – many regards
muerte – death
muerto – dead
mujer – woman
mujer lindísima – beautiful woman
multa – a monetary fine
muy – very
necesario – necessary
negro – black
nieta, nieto, los nietos – granddaughter, grandson, grandchildren
niña – girl
niño – boy
niños – children
no hay problema – no problem
nota – note
notaria, notario – notary (female, male)
noventa – 90
novia, novio – girlfriend, boyfriend
noviembre – November
nuestro, nuestros – our, ours
nueve – nine
océano – ocean
océano Pacifico – Pacific Ocean
ochenta – 80
ocho – 8
octubre – October
oficial – official
oficina – office
ojo – eye
once – 11

oración – prayer
orgánico – organic
ostiones – oysters
padre – father
palapa – open-air room with thatched roof
paletas – frozen treat similar to popsicles
panadería – bakery
panga – small open boat
papa – potato
Papá – dad
Papá Noel – Santa Claus
papas fritas – French fries
papel – paper
papel higiénico – toilet paper
parada – stop (noun)
parar – stop (verb)
pararse un alto – stop sign
parque – park
pasto – grass
peligroso – dangerous
pequeño – small
pera – pear
perdido – lost
perra, perro – dog (female, male)
pescado – fish (noun)
pescado a la parilla – fish cooked on the grill
pescadora, pescador – fisherwoman, fisherman
pescar – to fish
pico de gallo – spicy mix of tomatoes, onions, and peppers
piedra – stone
piña – pineapple
plátano – banana
plato – plate
playa – beach
poco cielo – little piece of sky
pollo – chicken
pollo con arroz – chicken with rice

polvo – dust
por favor – please
por qué? – why?
Precaución – caution
precio – price
preparado – ready
privada – private
problema – problem
propiedad – property
propina – monetary tip
público – public
puente – bridge
puerco – pork
puerta – door, doorway, gateway
puerto – port
punta – point of land
que – what
que pasa – what's happening?
queso – cheese
quince – 15
quinceañera – 15th birthday celebration
quinientos – 500
recámara – room
recibo – receipt
recompensa – reward
reparación – repair
rey – king
rico – rich
río – river
roca – rock
rojo – red
ropa – clothing
rostisado – roasted
sábado – Saturday
san, santo – saint
segunda – second
segunda mano – second hand

seguridad – safety
seguridado – security guard
seis – 6
semana – week
señor – Mr., gentleman
señora – Mrs., lady
señorita – Ms., young lady
separado – separate (adjective)
separarse – to separate (verb)
septiembre – September
sesenta – 60
setenta – 70
sierra – mountain range (literally, sierra is saw)
siete – 7
sin – without
soltera – single, unmarried
sombrero – hat or cap
sopa – soup
su – your (not a close relationship)
sur – South
tarjeta – card
tarjeta de crédito – credit card
tarjeta de Navidad – Christmas card
te amo – I love you
te extraño – I miss you
te, tu – you, your (a close relationship)
teléfono – telephone
tenedor – fork
ti pido discuplas – I apologize to you
tía, tío – aunt, uncle
tienda de abarottes – small grocery store
todo – all, everything
tope – speed bump
tostada – a flat toasted tortilla
trece – 13
tréinta – 30
trés – 3

treinta – 30
turista – tourist
un, una – a
uno – one
urgente – urgent
usted – you (formal, not a close relationship)
vado – dip in the road, usually at a shallow stream
valle – valley
vaqueros – cowboys
Vaya con Dios – Go with God
veinte – 20
veinticinco – 25
veinticuatro – 24
veintidós – 22
veintinueve – 29
veintiocho – 28
veintiséis – 26
veintisiete – 27
veintiuno – 21
vela – candle
velocidad – speed
verde – green
verdura – vegetable
viaje – trip
viejo – old; also old man
vientitrés – 23
viernes – Friday
vino – wine
vivo en México – I live in Mexico
y – and
yo – I
yo no habla español – I don't speak Spanish
zona – zone

I Love Baja!

Index

Index of People and Places. No last names except for authors and people in the public eye.

Made in the USA
Middletown, DE
06 July 2019